THE
EMPATHY
GAP

Daniel's work in this area and the insights he shares are without peer. His critical analysis of the topics he covers in The Empathy Gap are incredibly timely given the changes and challenges that leaders of business face. He brings to the conversation both an academic rigour and lived experience that is a rare and highly valued combination. I see this work of Daniel's as essential for leaders who want to better understand and importantly lead with empathy.

—**Peter Baines OAM,** bestselling author, keynote speaker, founder of Hands Across the Water

In an age of hyperpolarisation where people would rather than be correct than to be connected, empathy has never mattered more. In *The Empathy Gap*, Daniel Murray offers powerful insights for relearning the skill of seeing each other, hearing each other and learning from each other.

—**Michael McQueen,** bestselling author, trend forecaster and keynote speaker

THE
EMPATHY

THE BRIDGE TO
REAL CONNECTION
AND LASTING INFLUENCE

GAP

DANIEL MURRAY

WILEY

First published 2025 by John Wiley & Sons Australia, Ltd

© John Wiley & Sons Australia, Ltd 2025

ISBN: 978-1-394-33279-3

A catalogue record for this book is available from the National Library of Australia

Registered Office
John Wiley & Sons Australia, Ltd. Level 4, 600 Bourke Street, Melbourne, VIC 3000, Australia

For details of our global editorial offices, customer services, and more information about Wiley products visit us at www.wiley.com.

Cover design by Wiley
Cover Image: © MirageC/Getty Images

Set in 13/16pt Crimson Text by Straive, Chennai, India

Contents

Preface

On 12 September 2017, I found myself in an operating theatre in Sydney standing next to my wife, Miranda, as the doctors worked feverishly. I was terrified, grasping Miranda's hand and trying to reassure her that everything was going to be okay. Moments later, I heard the noise that changed my life forever. It was the first sound of our daughter, Zoe McKenzie Murray.

My terror in those moments wasn't just driven by the uncertainty of raising a child; Zoe had been a long time in the making. This was the tenth IVF Miranda had been through and after nine failures, we were deeply afraid that we'd feel the terrible pain of disappointment once again. If you have experienced this type of journey, or know someone who has, you will likely relate to the months of anticipation and preparation. The injections, the doctor visits and the long nights wondering if it will ever work out.

We were one of the lucky ones. Zoe is a healthy, happy little girl now who lights up our lives every day. She is cheeky, clever and already thinks genuinely about the feelings of other people, a trait undoubtedly imparted to her by her mother. While she is growing up very fast, we are loving every minute of the ride: from the scraped knees and snotty noses to the bedtime stories and warm hugs.

To be honest, I didn't really know if I'd be father material. My childhood didn't have a stable home life. Having witnessed two divorces and lived in many different homes, I wanted nothing more than to get away as a teenager. I went to university with no idea what I wanted to be. I studied a Bachelor of Science and majored in mathematics, less because of a passion and more because of the lack of reading involved.

I loved how mathematics was so logical and stable. Unlike my subjects in biology and chemistry, where variations and complexity made study essential, I found mathematics to be much more straightforward. Once you understand the rules, you just have to follow them. While the puzzles become more complicated, they never have bad days or change rules as a result of the weather.

During my university years, I took a job as a maths tutor for high-school students and loved it. I found it fascinating trying to work out how students think, how their minds see the world and how I could explain the world of mathematics to better fit their way of thinking. I then worked with younger children too, seeing the difference mild autism, Aspergers and other learning challenges had on the way children engaged with the world. The seed of empathy had been planted.

Despite my love for the work, the pay was terrible. I decided to try my hand in the corporate world, joining one of Australia's largest insurance companies and quickly climbing the ranks. I transitioned to the Commonwealth Bank and continued to hone my skills in navigating the world of corporate culture to eventually win the 2010 CBA CEO Award for my work inside the company and in the community.

The CBA sponsored my Masters of Business Administration through the Australian Graduate School of Management, seeing me as part of the talent pool to rise through the ranks and take on more leadership responsibility. This MBA gave me the credentials for leadership, strengthening my resume and improving my understanding of the technical skills required to manage a business. But then everything changed. After a divorce of my own, a few career changes and a stint running a large corporate foundation, I met Miranda and found the confidence to dive into my own space.

My decision to become a professional speaker, trainer and thought leader in the world of empathy would not have been possible without the support and wisdom of Miranda Murray. This book is dedicated to her patience, compassion and kindness. It is also inspired by our little Zoe. The world is a crazy place and bringing a new life into it is a great responsibility. I hope this book, and my work helping thousands of people become more empathic leaders, helps to create a better world for Zoe when she journeys beyond the nest.

INTRODUCTION
What if they don't want to do it?

The project plan laid out before us was a masterpiece of structure and organisation, a visual symphony of planning. One of the most intricate Gantt charts I had ever encountered graced the screen in front of us, complete with colour-coded work streams, milestones clearly delineated, and a comprehensive resource allocation table displaying an array of skillsets and roles categorised in neatly arranged columns and rows. Sitting alongside the project manager who owned this masterpiece, I saw a smile radiate pure pride and satisfaction.

My eyes were drawn to the resource allocation table. I had seen tables like this before. It was filled with figures representing the full-time equivalent (FTE) personnel assigned to each project activity. FTE is a term used in many organisations to symbolise the people allocated. These would be the individuals who would be pivotal to the project's success and here was a list of names followed by the numbers between 0.2 and 1. If someone was allocated fully in a week, they had a 1 in the FTE column as they would be fully dedicated. A 0.2 indicated they were only allocated for one day that week. I looked down the names and numbers and something stirred in my mind.

With my degree in mathematics, I certainly appreciate spreadsheets and numbers. But something about this table seemed lacking to me. I had been assigned to plenty of projects in my career, and they almost always had a good plan and Gantt charts like this one. But too often, they failed to deliver on time or within budget. We had brilliant PowerPoint decks, wonderful data sources and more than enough smart people on board, but still we underdelivered. Deadlines were missed, budgets blew out and issues that seemed small ballooned into massive challenges that caused the projects to grind to a halt. I had long wondered why.

Turning to the project manager, I posed a question that had been spinning in my mind for a while and that seemed straightforward on the surface.

'What if these people don't actually want to engage in the work?'

The question caught him off guard, his smile fading into a look of confusion. I elaborated further. 'You see, you have all these individuals assigned to tasks, assuming they'll work at a consistent, full-time level of productivity. But what if they don't? Take Bill Smith, for instance. I've worked with Bill before; he's a nice guy. Sometimes he's exceptionally productive, exceeding all expectations and knocking it out of the park. These times he is more like a 1.3. At other times, he is not. Bill isn't a fan of conflict and when people get pushy with him, he can really shut down. If I had to put a number on it, when times get really tense, Bill is more like a 0.2. Over the course of the project that feels like a bit of variation, so how do you factor in this level of variability?'

He looked back at me, still somewhat perplexed. He started to tell me about scoping documents they had prepared, routine meetings that were scheduled for the teams and detailed job descriptions that were drafted by incredibly expensive external consultants. I still wasn't convinced so he threw in a rather optimistic assumption that 'hopefully everyone will do their job'. As my good friend Peter Baines tells me, 'Hope is not a plan'.

I started to firmly believe that this was a fundamental reason why so many projects exceed their timelines and budgets. There will always be other factors like technology failures or equipment issues, but this basic expectation that people will perform like uniform, unvarying machines is completely flawed and we need to address it. Global consulting giant McKinsey has reported that on average, large IT projects overshoot their budgets by 45 per cent while delivering 56 per cent less value than anticipated. McKinsey also found that 17 per cent of IT projects fail so miserably that they could threaten the company's existence. A report by Procore found that 75 per cent of construction projects exceed their planned budgets, and 77 per cent are completed late.

Among various contributing factors, I am increasingly convinced that the key issue is our inability to effectively lead and manage people to elicit their optimal performance. People are inherently unpredictable in nature and can't be boiled down to a number. We are constantly being influenced by our surroundings, the people we work with and the many various pressures that affront us outside of work. Our workplaces are increasingly filled with pressure, stress and complexity that impacts different people in different ways on different days. With the rapid evolution of technology transforming industries and spawning new ones constantly, this change won't stop. We can't put on the brakes; we can't divide and conquer. To get the most out of each other, we need support.

This is why leadership is so crucial. By leadership, though, I am not referring only to the C-suite executives. So often, people think of leadership as the role of the most senior people in an organisation, but leadership is not a position. Leadership should be thought of as an integral capability throughout every division, team and work group. Merely issuing instructions from the top and hoping they trickle down correctly and flow through the processes of the organisation just isn't good enough to support performance in a complex modern world. The disconnect and complexity that often exist from the upper echelons to the front lines of an organisation leads to ambiguity and uncertainty. Exceptions to the norm arise, testing the strength of rigid processes and rules. Teams hit problems and need to be adaptive to the individual situation.

It's imperative that individuals at all levels feel supported, guided and empowered to discuss problems, manage challenges and make decisions to perform at their best. Every team member must have a clear understanding of their expected actions, behaviours and the outcomes they are responsible for. They also need to have support, people on hand to provide clarity and guidance, and timely feedback. Leadership can't be the responsibility of a select few; it must be a widespread, ingrained trait that stretches deep into every area within the group. There are few things worse than to find yourself completely lost at work and feel completely isolated. It is this feeling of being alone, even though you might be surrounded by a workplace full of people, that we need to address most of all. Isolation isn't just a physical condition.

Research by Michelle Lim and colleagues found that 34 per cent of Australians met criteria for episodic and chronic loneliness. Global health giant Cigna's research of 2500 people in the United States found 58 per cent felt lonely, with this number increasing for minority groups and lower income individuals.

More interestingly, younger generations of workers feel more alone, with the 18- to 22-year-old Gen Zs more than twice as likely as their 52- to 71-year-old Baby Boomer counterparts to feel abandoned and alienated by co-workers at work. Not surprisingly, the data also indicates that as the length of tenure for employees increases, the sense of loneliness decreases. How can we expect people to be firing on all cylinders when they feel isolated and unsupported by their colleagues?

Regrettably, as I found with my interaction with the project manager, individuals are frequently viewed merely as human resources. Sure, we all go to a conference or read a post on LinkedIn that says we should care about our people and foster a good culture. While many people do care sympathetically about their colleagues, sadly, when times are tough, it is all too common to see those human resources, the column of FTE on a spreadsheet, as a large expense that can be trimmed to meet some short-term financial targets. According to McKinsey, headcount reductions are the first step for more than half of all companies. When the pressure is on, people are expendable resources and more rigid and archaic forms of management seem to become prevalent.

In too many workplaces, despite the unique qualities and contributions people can offer, they are reduced to 'head count'. Just a name in a box on an organisational chart that can be crossed off. A body occupying a seat in an office that will soon be empty. People are treated as tangible assets, akin to any other physical resource. Like a printer we no longer want, we toss them out. However, as consulting company Bain & Company found in its analysis, sustained cost reduction requires a significant amount of coordination across different areas within and outside an organisation. Naturally, cutting out people too quickly will sever the relationships that may be vital for sustained cost-reduction to occur. Further, Bain and Company Partner, Peter Guarraia shared that it is people, especially at the frontline, who pose the biggest obstacle to sustaining long-term cost-reduction. How will we expect frontline people to feel when a wave of seemingly arbitrary cuts are made to friends and colleagues in their workplace?

The reality is we need to focus on the productivity of people as a variable that can alter substantially based on many factors. If a truck is running slow, it can be serviced; if a machine breaks down, it can be replaced. Such tangible assets can be monitored for performance using hundreds of sensors feeding large streams of data into computers to be analysed and actioned by reliability management professionals. These tangible assets are wonderful and when functioning well, offer highly predictable and consistent performance that we can easily forecast over time.

However, people aren't really like this at all. Human beings require more than just an occasional day off or monetary compensation to be at their best. If people feel stressed, tired, burned out, isolated, unsupported, inadequately equipped, poorly trained or mistreated by managers, colleagues or customers, the problems are sometimes difficult enough to identify, let alone to easily fix.

Consider the impact of someone expecting a promotion that was then given to a colleague they don't feel deserved it. In this circumstance, while from your perspective it might have been a good decision, in the eyes of our employee, they may feel resentful, that it isn't fair and maybe even that you are no longer a trustworthy manager in their eyes. Often, a grievance like this is not openly shared. Even if it is and you have the opportunity to explain your decision pragmatically, have you found that this does little to rectify the situation? Do they continue to do their best work? Go above and beyond for the team? Feel committed, supported and passionate about their work? An individual's response to such an experience is often complex, deeply personal and long-lasting.

The challenge we face in building, leading and performing as teams is immense. As organisations expand, this complexity increases exponentially. In the following pages, we will explore how developing trust, curiosity and understanding in our leaders and organisational culture is crucial to long-term, sustainable success. The leadership capabilities described enable leaders to manage a team's performance and productivity with confidence and certainty, rather than mere hope.

Leading a team isn't what it used to be

In ancient times, the role of a chief leading their tribe was crucial. The chief was more than just a leader; they were the heart of the tribe's customs, identity and values. They had the job of looking after the safety, wellbeing and survival of everyone in their group. Defending against threats while seeking new opportunities. Keeping the peace within the tribe and building relationships with nearby neighbours. Being a chief meant making decisions for the good of the tribe and building a culture and set of customs that kept the group alive.

Even though times have changed a lot, many of these qualities are still important in leadership today. However, there has been a significant shift in the types of people we need to lead. In today's business world, we aren't like tribal chiefs, who had the time to build relationships with their people over decades. Modern leaders are often tasked with pulling together a group of strangers to deliver immediate results. We rarely have the luxury of selecting people who understand our ways, practise our traditions and share our beliefs. Instead, we have to be able to bring together a variety of people from all sorts of backgrounds. Managing people is more challenging today because of the complexity diversity adds.

In its initial decades and well into the late 20th century, Toyota primarily employed Japanese staff. This choice stemmed from its goal to cultivate a uniform corporate culture and philosophy, deeply anchored in the Japanese traditions of 'Kaizen' (continuous improvement) and 'The Toyota Way'. Such practices were not unique to Toyota but were rather a hallmark of many Japanese firms during the post–World War II economic surge. Similarly, Qantas, in its earlier years, exclusively hired Japanese-born flight attendants for routes to Japan. On the other hand, Henry Ford, known for his diverse workforce, implemented an 'Americanization Program' at Ford Motor Company, aimed at integrating employees into a specific cultural framework.

The focus on these historical hiring practices might seem unexpected in a book about empathetic leadership, yet it underscores a crucial point: naturally forming and thriving in large, diverse teams is a challenge for humans. The concept of diversity, while now recognised as valuable, presents real and often overlooked challenges. For millennia, diversity was an unfamiliar idea, and our inherent abilities to manage it effectively are only still developing.

As a species, we evolved to live in small, highly social and largely homogenous groups. We called these groups tribes, and for thousands and thousands of years they were the dominant way humans survived and thrived. These tribes were small, tight-knit groups that were generally fiercely protective of their people, customs and beliefs. These tribes are the foundational structure for homo sapiens. We evolved as tribal animals working together to protect our group.

The massive challenge we face today is that we need to lead teams that look nothing like tribes. Modern teams are very different.

Today, we need to bring people from different backgrounds with completely different, often conflicting opinions and ideas together and motivate, coordinate and support them to achieve tasks that people just two generations ago would have thought impossible. The challenge for the modern leader is not if you need a more diverse team. It is how do you lead them effectively as a team?

The monkey and the rhino

To respond to the challenges of motivating these diverse teams, I have witnessed many organisations run campaigns focused on building resilience to sustain performance through the ups and downs of work. However, the implementation of the word 'resilience' was being misinterpreted by too many people I worked with. This led me to write a short kids' book dedicated to the diverse managers and employees working together through these challenges. Let me share the abridged version here (note: you can get a copy of the physical book on my website at www.empathicconsulting.com/our-kids-book or at most online book retailers):

In a far away land, stood a single, skinny, old tree on a hill. Under this tree lived a Rhino and a Monkey. They were very different. The Rhino was big and strong with a large horn on his nose. The monkey was small and fast and loved to climb, jump and leap around the tree. They were good friends.

The Monkey would climb to the top of the tree and pick the youngest leaves, which were the Rhino's favourite! The Rhino would protect the Monkey from the Lions who came around to scare him. Together the Monkey and the Rhino were a good team.

One day, dark clouds formed above the old skinny tree. A big storm was coming. They had never seen the clouds so dark before. First it started to rain, then large hailstones began to fall from the sky. The hail was very hard. Chunks of ice fell from the sky hitting the Monkey and the Rhino. Once the rain and hail had stopped, the Monkey sat on the ground in pain.

The hail had been very strong and hurt his little body. He had bumps and bruises on his arms and legs. The Monkey saw that the Rhino did not look hurt.

'Are you okay Mr. Rhino? Are you hurt from the hail like me?' asked the Monkey rubbing the bruises on his sore arms and legs.

'No, I am not hurt little Monkey,' said the Rhino. 'I am big and strong and tough. The hail can't hurt me. You need to toughen up little Monkey, you need thick skin like me!'

The Monkey thought the Rhino was right. He covered his skin in mud and sat in the sun to let it harden. He now had thick skin but he couldn't climb the tree. He couldn't pick the new leaves for his friend. He just lay in the sun baking, trying to get thick skin like the Rhino.

When the next dark clouds approached, the Monkey was sure he'd be okay. He did what the Rhino said. He now had thick skin. But the rain washed off the mud and the hail again crashed down on the monkey. The hail again battered and bruised the poor little Monkey.

The Monkey asked the Rhino, 'Why didn't it work? I tried to get thick skin just like you told me.'

The Rhino laughed. 'You just need to toughen up little Monkey, like me. You just have to have thick skin and nothing can hurt you!'

The Monkey was hurt and sad. He slumped back against the tree and started to cry. As he sat there, a small Squirrel popped his head out of a little hole in the tree.

'Are you okay Monkey?' asked the Squirrel.

'No, I am really hurt from the hailstones. They hurt me even after I tried to get thick skin,' said the Monkey. 'But you don't seem hurt Squirrel. Do you have thick skin like the Rhino?'

'No, no Monkey, I don't have thick skin like the Rhino,' said the Squirrel. 'We can't all have thick skin. I'm just small, so I hide in this little hole in the tree when the hail comes and I'm safe in here. We can't all have thick skin, but we can all find our own way to be safe from dangers.'

The little Monkey wondered how he could be safe. He looked at the small hole in the tree, but it was far too small for him to hide. He looked under a rock where the Ants were hiding from the hail, but it was far too small for him to fit under the rock. He thought he could hide in the lake with the fish, but he couldn't hold his breath for very long, so that wouldn't work. The Monkey found a hole in the ground, but it was very small and when he tried to squeeze inside, an angry badger came out to chase him away.

So the Monkey sat by the tree, looking all around him, wondering where he might be able to hide when the hail came. Then a big smile came across his little face!

As the next dark clouds appeared over the tree, and the rain started to fall, the Monkey wasn't scared. Before the hail came, the little Monkey walked over to his friend the Rhino. As the hail started to fall from the clouds, the Monkey walked across to his big friend and sat under the belly of the Rhino. There he was safe from the hail.

After the storm had passed, the Monkey said to the Rhino 'Thank you for the ideas Rhino. But I can't have thick skin like you. I just need to be me, small and fast so I can climb to the top of the tree to get the leaves for you. We can't all have thick skin,' said the Monkey. 'But we can all find a way to get by. If I had thick skin, I wouldn't be me!'

Too many managers, colleagues and friends share what I class as well-meaning rhino advice. We are too quick to tell people what we would do, or what we think would be best for them based on our perspectives. Far too few try to truly understand the unique strengths, weaknesses and perspectives before dishing this advice out. In an increasingly diverse world, we don't need more Rhinos, we need more empathic leaders.

Leaders must unlock the magic in diversity

This book is about helping leaders to build the critical skills they need to form, lead and manage performance in diverse teams. Well, actually it should help with any type of work relationship and in much of our personal lives too. Diversity is a wonderful and powerful gift of the modern world. I believe it is critical for us to continue to foster in order to survive and thrive in the future. While we are getting better at being near each other, I'm not sure we've even scratched the surface on how truly embracing diverse ideas can transform the world for the better.

We've never before faced the level of complexity and ambiguity that we face today. While many seek to divide us to support their own agenda, coming together is the only way we can meet the existential crises at our door successfully. The solutions of the past won't take us to the future; we can't make it great by going in reverse. The tribes we evolved from won't be the way forward; it will be new ways of connecting that will shape tomorrow. If you think your job as a leader is to build a team of like-minded people who get along and play nicely together, you are living in an ancient fantasy. Modern teams are challenging and should pull, push and stretch every member to become greater than they were before they joined. Individuals will shape teams and teams will shape individuals. It won't necessarily be comfortable, but it will be essential.

I have experienced the beauty and power of diversity on my own travels. The French writer Marcel Proust once said, 'The real voyage of discovery consists not in seeking new landscapes but in having new eyes'. That's been my experience journeying into new places. Whether hiking high mountains in China and Nepal, cycling through villages in Vietnam, Thailand and France, exploring the ancient caves of central Turkey, exploring the chaotic beauty of Moroccan souks or just relaxing in a small pub on the Isle of Skye, for me travelling has been about more than seeing new places. It's about meeting different people, experiencing their way of life, and letting it change how I see and think about the world. Diversity is beautiful and these different experiences shape our brains. Our assumptions are tested: some are falsified, others confirmed. These experiences challenge us, change us and equip us with new perspectives with which to move forward.

When you have a team with people from different cultures, places and backgrounds, you have the potential to open doors to amazing new ideas. If cultivated, this unique combination of skills can be harnessed to create new solutions to complex problems. When different people cooperatively collaborate it can lead to solutions no one person could have dreamed up on their own. Diverse teams can be unstoppable forces of adaptivity and performance.

However, it is not as simple as putting them in a room and hoping for the best. Diversity can also be a recipe for explosive destruction. Diverse teams can become overwhelmed by their differences. Different communication styles can lead to miscommunication and misunderstanding. Assumptions and biases can cause some members of diverse teams to feel less valued or included. Factions can form and relationships become pressured. While the promise of diversity is a world of greater opportunity, it can also be a petri dish perfect for cultivating high levels of conflict, animosity and distrust.

A successful leader is able to bring together different people; foster trusted and committed relationships between them that empower each person to share their ideas constructively; debate and explore with fearless curiosity; and foster a culture of inclusion, collaboration and performance. They are able to unleash the power of diversity without it exploding into chaos. A good leader is fascinated with understanding individual differences and able to nurture these different perspectives in a way that supports collective performance. A good leader knows the triggers and situations that create tension and walks the tightrope of managing the constructive conflict and challenging of ideas in a positive way.

Dealing with old hardware

One of the real and underappreciated challenges for modern leaders is that our brains are sophisticated and amazing, but are also old hardware. Our best estimates based on modern scientific analysis suggest the human brain hasn't changed much in the last 10 000 years. While the complexity of the concepts we can consider and the volume of knowledge we can retain may have increased exponentially, the size, structure and capacity of modern brains are incredibly similar to our very ancient ancestors.

These ancient brains evolved over longer periods of time and, through natural selection, were shaped to be amazingly useful pieces of biological equipment. They allowed us to harness a diverse range of tools and technology, share these through communication and language, adapt rapidly to different climates and environments, and form complex social groups that spread across the planet. The brain is the centre of human brilliance:

from innovation to creativity and communication, this 1.3-kilogram ball of fats, water and protein is one of the most complex systems in the known universe. You are very lucky to have one — congratulations!

However, brains weren't really designed to have to learn new habits, beliefs and ideas from the vast numbers of different people we might encounter throughout our modern lifetimes. For most of human history, we learned all the customs and beliefs from the people who surrounded us early in our childhoods. These were carried by stories, traditions and rituals and passed on to the next generation of the tribe, creating a unique culture that was reinforced over generations. Ancient humans had to learn the ways of the small number of people around them and build trusted relationships within this small group.

Ancient humans never needed to learn the ways of hundreds or even thousands of strangers who thought very differently, had different customs or held beliefs that completely contradicted their own. Interactions with these types of people would have been incredibly rare and fleeting. Ancient humans had their tribe and its tribal ways, some of which didn't always mix well with others of differing ideas. European explorers of the 15th and 16th centuries regularly found initial hospitalities turned to hostility over seemingly minor differences in custom or tradition. Many of these conflicts ended in horrific outcomes for all involved. In times of the past, people who thought differently from the tribe were likely ousted to maintain harmony within the group. While it is tempting to think this is a relic of the past, it still lives strongly within us today. This tribal instinct has not subsided and in many ways may be stronger than ever.

While the more radical versions such as nationalism, extremism and cults might come to mind immediately, this conforming to group can be seen in more subtle ways — for example, common phrases in organisations, such as:

- Keep the peace
- Let sleeping dogs lie
- Don't rock the boat
- Pick your battles
- Play nice.

These all point to the prioritisation of social cohesion above all else. It is in our nature to build and protect our tribe, but it doesn't always serve us. We need to move past this instinct, even if it is hard. Being in a large, diverse group is not something that comes naturally to many people. Being open, honest and comfortable to push against the social norms of the group can be challenging and dangerous.

Imagine walking into a large party where you don't know anyone. Most people will feel a sense of uncertainty and vulnerability. Many people fear rejection and worry about other people's impressions and opinions of them. There is a small number of people who will embrace this challenge, especially if motivated by opportunity or emboldened by a few drinks. Some people will simply turn around and leave. The majority will stay but will seek out someone familiar to engage with first. Someone who looks like 'your people'. It could be someone wearing the types of clothes you wear. Someone who is speaking your language, even better if it is with your accent. We look for safety in similarity. Homogeneity, even if this is misguided, is our default.

For most of history, people looked for people who saw the world the way they did and protected the social cohesion of the tribe if it was threatened. This is something we still see all over the world today. Different groups with their own special clothes, dances, music and language. We form groups on the internet who like what we like and connect with them, share ideas and reinforce beliefs. We become members of groups, feel connected to them and identify as 'one of them'. From fishing enthusiasts to political groups, conspiracy theorists to people who like dressing up as cats, people actively go out to seek people who are like them to form a tribal connection.

When forming a new team at work, we often gravitate towards people with whom we share interests and get along. These people are easy for us to understand and see the world in similar ways. We naturally find it is easier to strike up a conversation with someone who does the same kind of work as we do. There is an instant topic with significant depth with which to start a conversation you can both actively participate in. If you see someone wearing your favourite football team's jersey, you can connect pretty fast.

At work, we often hear the words 'cultural fit' used in selecting candidates, but too often we're just looking for people who are enough like us that they'll fit in easily. They won't challenge the norms here; they won't rock the boat. We can easily picture them being one of us and it will be easy. Our tribal brains like this simple shortcut because it builds a sense of safety and predictability into what can be a very uncertain situation. Bringing in the wrong person might mess up what we already have, so we play it safe. But this is misguided. We need to rock the boat now more than ever before in human history.

Teams that are made up of people who all think the same way are often highly content and collegiate, but are generally not as good at coming up with new ideas or adapting to change. Research by Anita Wooley from the Tepper School of Business has found that while homogenous teams might score higher on team engagement, this doesn't at all correlate to greater collective intelligence or problem solving. It is the ability to bring a diverse, more socially sensitive group together that delivers the best results.

It might feel nice and safe to be surrounded by like-minded people, but shared thoughts and beliefs can also create shared limitations on the range of ideas that can be generated. When a team is more focused on playing nice to maintain the cohesion, it often prioritises conformity over progress. This spells the beginning of the end for most teams. When responses are not adaptive and outcomes fail to be delivered, all the collegiate niceness and employee harmony might not keep you together. Engagement is nice but it is consistent performance that is required to survive in a competitive modern world.

Homogeneity was fine in the past partly because it was the only option. You couldn't quickly pull together a group of people from all corners of the world when your only mode of transport was walking and communication was by spoken word. Proximity was the limiting factor to diverse groups. Today's world gives us a chance to work with all kinds of different people, from every corner of the world, all the time. The challenge is how do we talk to, understand and, importantly, actively disagree with people who are so different from us? How do we lead a team like that? How do we bring people together and foster trusted relationships? How do you manage the complexities of a diverse team and get people who see the world in totally different ways to work together effectively?

The answer is leading with empathy. Being an empathic leader means really understanding where people are coming from, even if they're very different from you. Empathy is about finding out what drives them. Not only what their ideas are, but also what the things are that created those ideas. What motivates them as a person? We need to know what they love; what they hate; what lights them up and drives them to pour blood, sweat and tears into their work. If you want to lead a high-performance team, you need to sustainably get the best out of everyone. That involves understanding the uniqueness of each person and finding ways to bring them together into a committed force.

This book will help you understand how to do just that. It's all about seeing your own biases, learning how to connect with different kinds of people and building a team culture that delivers. If you're looking to learn how to lead diverse teams, this book is right for you. So let's dive in!

CHAPTER 1

Understanding the cognitive challenges of empathy

I vividly remember the excitement of starting my first major management consulting project. I had freshly arrived in the big smoke of Sydney from little old Brisbane and found myself part of a small team tasked with a colossal challenge. We had been asked to organisationally redesign the Australian arm of a global insurance behemoth. The company had grown rapidly through acquisitions, yet had largely ignored the potential synergies across its diverse business units by integrating them operationally. Our goal was simple: thoroughly investigate and propose ways to restructure the business to enhance operational efficiency and reduce the company's sprawling number of siloed divisions into a leaner, more effective structure.

This was also my first project as a management consultant and I was in awe of the incredible intellect and talent of my colleagues. They effortlessly crafted voluminous, sophisticated PowerPoint decks brimming with graphs, charts and diagrams that mapped out a clear path through the labyrinth of opportunities. In only a few days we had crafted a 'master plan document' that was nothing short of an awe-inspiring journey from the current state through to a utopian future. The seasoned consultants seemed to possess an intuitive grasp of the company's complexities, visualising a streamlined future marked by consolidation of resources and efficiency of output. The prospect of massive cost savings, well into the tens of millions annually, added a tangible sense of excitement to our mission. This was a big piece of work!

With the master plan document finalised, our immediate task was to engage with the company's senior leaders and gather their initial feedback. Meetings were scheduled and each of us was assigned to attend sessions with the executives from the different divisions. My meeting was with a gentleman we affectionately nicknamed 'the Walrus', due to his large, burly build and prominent, bushy moustache. In his early 60s, the Walrus managed a highly specialised team who serviced large corporate clients. My previous encounters with him had been limited to brief sightings in the office corridors, where he strode with the confident, unbothered air of a grizzly bear, invariably dressed in a pinstriped suit and a bold red tie that signalled his sense of power.

Given the high stakes of these meetings, we opted for a buddy system. I was to partner with one of the senior consultants for an 8.30 am meeting on a Tuesday. Keen to make a good impression, I had arrived at the office by 7.30 am, carefully reviewing the master plan document. I meticulously highlighted key phrases, circled critical figures and scribbled footnotes to ensure I was across all the essential points.

At 8.09 am, my phone rang. It was the senior consultant I was meant to be going to the meeting with. Due to unforeseen personal circumstances, they couldn't make it into the office until 8.45 am at the earliest. I asked if we should reschedule, but the tightness of our timeline meant any delay could jeopardise the entire project. They suggested I start the meeting solo, with the assurance that they would join as soon as possible. We had set aside 45 minutes for the meeting so they'd be there for the second half, which is when we expected most of the questions and conversation to happen anyway.

Armed with three copies of the master plan document, I arrived at the Walrus' office early, eager to be as prepared as possible. His assistant ushered me to an uncomfortably rigid chair by his office door. As I sat there, I nervously flipped through the documents, reinforcing the key points in my mind while casting hopeful glances towards the door for my colleague to arrive. Alas, they were nowhere to be seen.

At precisely 8.30 am, I was summoned by the Walrus' assistant. It was time. The Walrus sat behind a large, imposing wooden desk, framed by shelves laden with leather-bound books, industry awards and photographs from various events. He glanced up, casually pushed his keyboard aside and gestured for me to sit.

'Is it just you?' he enquired with surprise in his voice, interlacing his fingers and leaning forward in his chair.

I nodded, muttering that my colleague's arrival had been delayed due to traffic and personal issues. My hands trembled as I retrieved the copy of the master plan document printed for him from its sleeve and handed it across the desk. Without hesitation, I launched into the prepared presentation, outlining the reengineering program we proposed, the major streams of work envisaged and our future structure for the company. Focused intently on my notes, I rattled off relevant industry benchmarks, pointing out charts and figures that highlighted the great opportunities we had identified. I could feel my heart racing, but my thorough preparation seemed to be paying off as

I confidently echoed the key phrases and taglines used regularly by the senior consultants during team discussions.

After a few minutes that felt like hours, I paused to ask if he had any questions. Immediately, I knew something was very wrong. Lifting my gaze, I saw he hadn't even opened the document I had handed to him. The expression across his face was not interest or excitement, but sheer rage. His eyes, piercing and intense, looked straight into my soul. His lips seemed to convey a silent, furious disdain for every word I had uttered until now. Then, without warning, he slammed his hand down on the desk, the sound echoing throughout the room.

'This is a complete waste of my time. You've done nothing but waste my time so far. I have only one question: *When are you going to stop wasting my fucking time?*' he thundered in a booming voice.

I stammered a stunned apology, hastily gathered the papers into my case and hurried out of the office. The assistant bid me a sheepish goodbye, clearly hearing what had gone on inside, but I was too embarrassed to even look back. My head bowed as I walked briskly out of the building and made my way to a nearby café. Slumping into a corner seat, I sent a text message to the other consultant: 'Don't bother coming, the meeting's over. Nightmare. We'll talk later'.

As I sat there sipping a coffee, the gravity of what had just happened began to sink in. My confidence was shattered. My reputation was destroyed. My head ached with the echo of his booming voice. It couldn't have gone any worse. I felt sick in my stomach.

After some time, a colleague from the team tracked me down and joined me in the café. I told her what had happened.

'Yeah, I heard. What an arsehole. Don't worry about him. He is a corporate dinosaur more interested in bullying people into submission than being a good leader,' she said comfortingly. 'He isn't going to be around too long anyway. His division will be one of the first we will cut up into little pieces and he will be retiring to become a grumpy old man on a golf course somewhere. Don't stress.'

For many years I believed my colleague's explanation. I thought about the incident as purely his fault. He was the Walrus, a nasty piece of work. It wasn't my fault. I reflected on this many times during the months after and most times would quickly dismiss the whole episode as a grumpy old corporate dinosaur taking out his frustration on the innocent kid. What a bully! But as the years wore on and my reflections of that day shifted, eventually I realised that this simple explanation was wrong.

It wasn't him. I was the problem.

My encounter with the Walrus wasn't just a harsh lesson in the way consultants are sometimes treated by senior executives. The reality was that despite my meticulous preparation of our materials and the genuine thought sitting within the master plan document, my approach was deeply flawed. In the lead-up to the meeting, I had focused too much attention in the wrong place. All my preparation was on our work, our objectives and what we wanted from him. I concentrated on what I was going to say, what the external benchmarks suggested and how we saw the future. I wrongly thought everything that mattered sat on the pages of our document. I had forgotten the most important piece: I hadn't once thought about him.

We must become adept at blending our hard analytical thinking with the intangible skills of emotional intelligence, perspective-taking and leading with empathy.

My approach lacked a critical element of all genuine conversations: empathy. I had failed to consider how our plan would be received by the person sitting across from me. I didn't at all understand his worries, hopes, priorities or concerns. I had ignored the implications of this plan on his clients, his partners and his people. The Walrus had spent more than 30 years in the industry building relationships, friendships and a reputation. This program was going to threaten all of it. To him, our 'master plan' was a siege on his empire and my approach suggested that we were doing it to him, not with him. I had known what I wanted *from* him, but not at all what I wanted *for* him.

Though initially demoralising, the meeting with the Walrus became a turning point in my career. Over time, the incident felt more like a lesson that helped me to understand the importance of empathy in the workplace. This has now become a lesson I seek to share with other workplaces and people leaders around the globe. It's not to say we don't need the more technical skills of our professions — of course we need an ever-growing depth of expertise. But we also need to deepen our ability to understand the human behind the skills and create relationships of trust and commitment to succeed. As more groups of diverse people are required to come together to successfully navigate the complex waters of our modern world, we must become adept at blending our hard analytical thinking with the intangible skills of emotional intelligence, perspective-taking and leading with empathy.

We must always remember, organisations don't exist without people. Whether an employee, customer, constituent, partner or shareholder, all organisations are developed to serve humans in some way. For this reason, we must always understand that true leadership in any organisation — from corporate to government, small business to not-for-profit — lies in understanding the impact the leader's activity has on the lives of people.

If you expect them to fix it, expect to be disappointed

Although my colleague in the consulting team might still argue that the Walrus was to blame, another lesson I learned from the experience is that we cannot expect others to change and do things as we would prefer them to be done. It's easy to say he should have acted more kindly, but the fact is, he didn't. There could have been an endless number of reasons he acted the way he did that had little or nothing to do with my performance in the meeting. It's easy to view the situation as a single interaction, but the world is far more complex. Blaming him was easy, but it wasn't useful.

This is an all-too-common mistake we make as humans. In psychology, it's referred to as 'projection'. In the context of conflict, it refers to an unconscious psychological defence mechanism where an individual attributes their own unwanted emotions, desires or impulses onto someone else. This often happens when our feelings are considered unacceptable or uncomfortable to acknowledge. Personally admitting fault about the situation may threaten our ego and sense of self. Projecting the blame onto the other person is like a mental trick designed to shield us from the guilt and shame. I had felt terrible embarrassment at the Walrus' response. Blaming him for being a mean person helped me to feel it wasn't my fault. But this is wrong.

Projection as a tactic in conflict is fundamentally flawed because it distorts your perception of reality. The muddying of the waters impacts the accuracy of your memory and makes it more difficult to objectively reflect and identify the underlying root causes of the issue. It shifts the focus from internal introspection to external accusation, creating a barrier to genuine resolution. By projecting, we avoid confronting our own insecurities, vulnerabilities and responsibilities. This evasion hampers the resolution of the conflict, creating a divide between people by focusing on alternative subjective experiences of a situation rather than objective facts. Consistent projection also stunts our own emotional development, shielding us from the sometimes painful exercise of self-criticism and analysis that leads to greater self-awareness.

This skill of accurately assessing our actions, emotions and responses is crucial in building healthy relationships as it enables the understanding of behaviours and triggers, which in turn fosters better interactions with others. Dr Tasha Eurich, an organisational psychologist and researcher, emphasises that self-awareness is a foundational component for effective leadership and personal relationships. Her research indicates that individuals who possess a high degree of self-awareness are better at managing their emotions and understanding the perspectives of others, which leads to more meaningful and resilient connections. By being self-aware, individuals can navigate conflicts more effectively, build trust, and create a supportive environment where both parties feel valued and understood.

Taking personal accountability is a cornerstone of humility, emotional intelligence and maturity. When individuals own their actions, behaviours, thoughts, feelings and attitudes, they foster a climate of honesty and reliability with those around them. Accountability encourages a direct approach to problem solving, where each person's contribution to a conflict is recognised and addressed. It allows for constructive criticism and deeper self-reflection, which, when embraced, can lead to personal and interpersonal growth.

Moreover, taking personal accountability empowers us as individuals to make positive changes. When we acknowledge our role in a situation, we can take active steps towards improvement. As Paulo Coelho, famous author of *The Alchemist* said, 'It's always easy to blame others. You can spend your entire life blaming the world, but your success and failures are entirely your own responsibility'.

Taking accountability not only helps resolve conflicts more effectively but also builds resilience and coping strategies for the future. Additionally, by modelling accountability, we encourage others to do the same, creating a more cooperative and supportive environment.

In essence, projection is a defence mechanism that perpetuates a cycle of blame and misunderstanding, while personal accountability breaks that cycle, leading to growth, improved relationships and the resolution of conflicts. Remembering that the problem might begin with you is a useful way to view any situation through as a starting point. I'm not suggesting you are always at fault, but starting analysis from the perspective of your own actions and contributions to the situation is better than jumping to point fingers. It's common to find that our own complexities and imperfections have played at least some role, and by working on them, we can learn, grow and be more effective both in the moment and in the future.

Why is empathy so damn hard?

I want you to imagine someone named Sam.

Sam is quiet and helpful but is generally withdrawn socially and has little interest in people. Sam is meek, tidy and loves things to be structured and orderly. Sam prefers studying the details over exploring new ideas. Sam lives in Australia. Based on this description, if you had to guess which of the following was Sam's profession, which would you choose:

- airline pilot

- farmer

- librarian

- physician.

Did you guess that Sam was a librarian? If so, you are not alone. Famous research conducted by psychologists Amos Tversky and Daniel Kahneman found that in examples similar to this one, up to 95 per cent of participants made a similar assumption. But why do so many choose the librarian? It's most likely they all employed a similar heuristic. Heuristics are mental shortcuts or rules of thumb used by our brains to make decisions. Our brains didn't evolve with the luxury of spare time, energy or opportunity to solve problems from first principle analysis in every situation. Instead, we look for easier ways to make decisions based on our past knowledge and experiences. If it looks like a duck, swims like a duck and quacks like a duck, then it probably is a duck.

These heuristics and mental models save us incredible amounts of mental capacity and are very dangerous. As Kahneman describes them in his groundbreaking book *Thinking, Fast and Slow*, a heuristic is 'a simple procedure that helps find adequate, though often imperfect, answers to difficult questions'. Being useful doesn't mean it is accurate. An example might be that being out in cold weather gives you a cold. Many parents will tell their child to wear warmer clothes and stay indoors to avoid getting sick. While cold air can add stress to the immune system and dry the mucous membranes in the throat making us more susceptible to a cold, a cold is actually caused by exposure to the cold virus.

While keeping warm and indoors might indirectly help in some ways, cold weather doesn't cause a cold. Also, if you are staying indoors with other people who are carrying the virus, you'll be more likely to catch a cold.

Thinking back to the description of Sam, most people will compare the information they had against existing stereotypes of the four different occupations shown. Most people chose the librarian because they feel the description of quiet, helpful, meek and tidy better fits their assumptions about that job compared to the other options. Libraries are quiet places; staff are helpful and they regularly sort books to be neat, tidy and in the right places. The brief description of Sam nicely fits their stereotype of a librarian.

While the descriptions fit, it is statistically a terrible guess. What you should have also considered is the size of the respective number of people who do these jobs. There are many, many more farmers and physicians in Australia than there are librarians: roughly 10 to 13 times as many. The total pool of Australian librarians is around 10 000. The number of physicians is around 130 000 and the number of farmers is closer to 135 000. Imagine you have a jar with 130 red balls, 135 green balls and only 10 yellow balls. If you pulled one out at random, there is a 47 per cent chance of it being red, 49 per cent chance of green and only just over 3 per cent chance it would be yellow.

You should have guessed that Sam is a physician or farmer; it is statistically much more likely. Moreover, there are plenty of quiet, helpful, meek and tidy people who become farmers and physicians. If only 10 per cent of farmers or physicians fit this description, it would still be more than all the librarians in Australia. The problem is our brains like to see patterns, use heuristics and ignore the more abstract concepts of statistics.

The librarian heuristic is strong, while the much more relevant population data is not known or ignored. The description just feels right, even though it was likely wrong.

Heuristics are a double-edged sword. On one hand they offer speed, efficiency and utility; on the other they can lead to assumptions, errors and poor choices. They allow you to react instantly in many situations: accurately predicting where to put your hands to catch a ball, when to brake when driving a car or what to do if someone yells 'duck'. However, the same mechanisms that make heuristics advantageous also lead to bias and distortions in more important situations requiring critical reasoning. This underscores the intricate interplay between cognitive efficiency and vulnerability. Your brain is an extraordinary piece of equipment, but it is not perfect.

In *Thinking, Fast and Slow*, Kahneman describes the brain as having two systems: system 1 and system 2. These systems provide a useful model for the way we think and make decisions. System 1 operates automatically and quickly, with little effort and low levels of voluntary control. This system relies heavily on heuristics, emotions and instincts. System 1 is incredibly efficient at processing everyday tasks and making quick decisions based on limited information. It is brilliant at pattern recognition, routine actions and what we consider multitasking. System 1 can be incredibly powerful, but its reliance on shortcuts can lead to oversimplifications and mistakes, as we have seen.

System 2, on the other hand, is the more analytical, deliberative and systematic processing function of our brain. We use this to solve complex problems, deliberate over factual data and exert more self-control. System 2 is the centre of the rational, sequential processing that we use in deep and focused work. Halving a number is often done by system 1, long division by system 2.

The downside of this system is that it is much slower, requiring more effort, energy and concentration to engage. Engaging system 2 can put significant strain on our cognitive resources and we look to limit the amount of information we need to take in. Have you ever found that you can drive and listen to music without any issue, but when you need to reverse park you turn the radio off? This is system 2 looking to reduce the input to increase focus.

System 2 is often only called into action when we recognise a task as challenging. When needing to concentrate, assess evidence or think through a difficult decision more methodically we fire up these cognitive networks for action. While system 2 can override the impulses and biases of system 1, it demands a significant amount of energy, and humans naturally tend to conserve metabolic resources. Our brains already consume a huge amount of our body's energy. While only about 2 per cent of our body weight, they consume around 20 per cent of its total energy and we are not designed to use excessive amounts of energy frivolously.

This means, by default, system 1's automatic judgements are in control most of the time, with the power-hungry deliberations of system 2 reserved for special occasions. System 1 uses the description of Sam and matches it with existing heuristics to pick librarian. System 2 would have been required for the research and calculation of probability to make the more accurate choice of farmer or physician.

We have been talking about Sam and what their occupation is for a while now, but before we move on, I have one final request. I want you to create an image of Sam in your mind. As a librarian, what clothes are they wearing? What does their face look like? What haircut do they have? Based on everything I've shared about Sam so far, have you inadvertently assumed Sam's gender too? While it could be considered a controversial topic for some people, it is also very likely that you made an assumption on when you formed your mental image. Our brains are very good at making predictive assumptions, collating them with other information we have at our disposal, then using them as data to make decisions.

This is at the heart of why empathy is so challenging and important. Brains are brilliant at finding patterns, even when they aren't really there. We find correlations and assume causation. We often jump to conclusions based on limited information, relying on simple models to make sense of the complexity of reality. This cognitive shortcut, while efficient for some tasks, falls short when used to understand other people. We need system 2 for empathy.

Empathy requires effort

Despite the need for it increasing, empathy is in shorter supply than we would want in today's world: it takes a lot of effort. Empathy gets its etymological roots from the Greek word *empathes*, meaning 'feeling into'. There are many formal definitions of empathy, from affective or emotional empathy—which relates to an ability to share someone else's emotional state—to somatic empathy which, is a more physical response to the emotional state of another. For the purposes of this book, we will focus on the definition of empathy in clear and simple terms: *understanding why people do what they do.* This is more closely related to cognitive empathy and is recognised as a critical skill in effective communication, social interaction and problem solving in interpersonal relationships.

The focus for our ability to lead, manage and work with others is the intellectual ability to recognise and understand another person's perspective or mental state. It is the awareness of the other person's drivers, motives and ideas, which allows for more effective communication and social interaction without necessarily involving personal emotional alignment or engagement.

Contrastingly, emotional empathy involves directly feeling the emotions another person is experiencing, creating a deeper, more visceral form of understanding and connection. In leadership and team situations, this can become encumbering and even debilitating when needing to make decisions. Emotional stress can empower system 1 to react and reduce the ability to make clear, system-2-led decisions. This is why the focus of this book will be on the cognitive skills of empathy and its practical application in workplaces. This is not to say emotions can or should be ignored. Emotions still play a huge role in all human interactions — we just want to be more aware of their involvement rather than allowing them to overly influence our actions and decisions.

The exploration of empathy as a psychological and philosophical concept has evolved over centuries, with its formal study gaining momentum in the early 20th century. Modern psychology suggests empathy as an essential component of human connection, enabling individuals to bridge the gap between separate experiential worlds. There have even been some neurological studies suggesting human brains — and those of some other complex, social animals — are designed to experience empathy.

Back in the early 1990s, neurophysiologist Giacomo Rizzolatti and his team at the University of Parma, Italy stumbled upon a curious phenomenon in the brains of macaque monkeys. They found that certain neurons in the premotor cortex fired not just when the monkeys reached for something themselves, but also when they watched another do the same action. They called these 'mirror neurons' as they seemed to mimic observed behaviour as if it were their own. This effect wasn't just unique to monkeys; fMRI studies showed that the same regions of the brains of humans activated when people both watched and imitated certain facial expressions. While research is ongoing, there is some evidence that this might be the fundamental way we connect, communicate and comprehend other people.

These neurons seem to bridge the gap between seeing and doing, and allow us to step into another's shoes. Mirror neurons have the promise that our ability to empathise, comprehend language and grasp others' intentions might just be rooted in the innate act of neural mimicry. It's as if these neurons are the brain's way of doing a little internal role-play, allowing us to better understand the subtleties of others inside the confines of our own mind.

This concept — that our brains can essentially mirror the actions we observe, creating a silent symphony of understanding and connection — has been seen as revolutionary. However, the research and implications have not been without criticism. Even if these mirror neurons help to simulate the experience of someone else, the key underlying question still remains: Is our interpretation of their experience in any way close to the actual experience they are having? It is one thing to see someone banging their shin into a coffee table and accurately imagining the feeling of pain in our own shin. If I observe someone crippled with grief from the loss of a spouse, will I be able to innately mimic their complex emotional response with the same accuracy?

This is one of the central questions to keep in mind as we explore the role of empathy in leadership and teams. Just because we think we understand why someone does what they do, doesn't mean we are correct. As the situations become more complex and the diversity of human experience increases, this will potentially become even more difficult. Like the heuristics we used to determine Sam was a librarian, our mirroring relies on our own experiences as the simple shortcuts to understand others.

Mirroring is certainly a useful ability, but we also need intentional tools that we can use to override these automatic, system-1 processes.

Earlier in our relationship, my darling wife would ask me, seemingly out of the blue, 'What's wrong?' It was a pointed question, usually said with a tone of worry that would catch me off guard while I was deep in thought. Most of the time my honest answer was that nothing was wrong, and I was surprised that she was asking with such concern. She would then say, 'It's that look on your face. Something is wrong. What's up?'

If this has happened to you, you will likely know the feeling of utter confusion I would have felt. From my perspective, nothing was *wrong*. I was thinking deeply about something — a problem or scenario — but I was not upset, unhappy or disgruntled in any way. What was going on with my face that made her think something was wrong when I felt like nothing was wrong at all?

What was happening is called 'misattribution of emotion'. This occurs when one inaccurately assumes the emotional state of another based solely on facial cues. As humans, we study the faces of others very closely. Studies have shown that when asked to observe others, people spend almost 80 per cent of their time focusing on the face and can pick up on micro-expressions that last for only a small fraction of a second. For many basic emotions, people are fairly accurate at determining the emotions of another person based on their facial expressions, but this becomes more challenging as the diversity of the people and complexity of emotions increase.

Using facial expressions alone — without considering context, verbal cues or other nonverbal signs — is a key cause of misattribution. The misunderstandings and miscommunications caused can be entertaining and are regular features of movies and television shows. From the deadpan expressions of Wednesday Addams, the apparent awkwardness of Spock on *Star Trek* and the emergence of the term 'resting bitch face', misattribution is something we both well understand and consistently perform. Anxiety and restlessness could be misinterpreted as frustration. Determination can be seen as hostility. A glint in someone's eye could be hopefully read as a sign of attraction when it was really caused by dust, embarrassment or fear.

As for my wife, she was misreading the physical signs of concentration with those of concern. Of course, if this has happened to you, you may also have found that simply explaining to the other person that this is a misinterpretation on their part rarely resolves the issue. Quite often, the person who has misinterpreted will suspect that they are correctly interpreting the situation and become suspicious that something is being concealed. Rejecting the misinterpretation can create additional misinterpretation. In my wife's case, she still regularly *tells me* that I am in a grumpy mood when I am actually just deep in concentration. Her comments alone are sometimes enough to make me grumpy when I wasn't before, which frustratingly makes her right! Oh, the wicked webs we weave.

Do you know what you want?

Accurately interpreting the mind of another is incredibly difficult. Our brain is the centre of our world and the hub of our decision-making processes. However, the drivers of our decisions are not always consciously available to us. The human brain is a fascinatingly complex structure that we are only just beginning to understand. We can't see what someone else is thinking and don't always know why we do what we do, which makes other people being able to know for sure incredibly difficult.

One breakthrough in brain research happened in the wake of radical medical procedures first performed in 1939 at the University of Rochester Medical Center, which offered an interesting insight into how different regions of the brain communicate internally. The operation, called a 'corpus callosotomy', is a neurosurgical procedure that involves severing the corpus callosum, the major bundle of neural fibres connecting the left and right hemispheres of the brain. This operation was performed on a number of people suffering severe, intractable epilepsy that could not be controlled with medication.

The primary objective of the corpus callosotomy was to reduce the frequency and severity of epileptic seizures. Epilepsy is a neurological disorder characterised by recurrent, unprovoked and sometimes debilitating seizures. In some patients, seizures originate in one hemisphere of the brain and spread to the other hemisphere via the corpus callosum, exacerbating the severity of the seizures. Cutting the corpus callosum significantly reduced the spread of epileptic activity from one hemisphere to the other, thereby controlling the seizures more effectively. This can be life changing, allowing patients to engage more fully in daily activities and reducing the risk of injury from seizures.

In addition to providing patients with this limited relief, it also provided researchers with some unique opportunities to study the way the brain worked. Between 1962 and 1967, Roger Sperry and Michael Gazzaniga at the California Institute of Technology had the opportunity to study patients who had received a corpus callosotomy — not in the impact on their seizures, but on how their now separate brain hemispheres processed information and communicated.

There are also some significant differences between the two hemispheres of the brain and while there are many functions in the brain that are processed across both hemispheres, some are more localised. The left hemisphere controls all the right side of the body and tends to hold most of the processing of language, speech, sequential processing, analytical thinking and details. The right hemisphere controls the left side of the body along with the centre for creativity, imagination, spatial abilities and intuitive thinking. In most people, this means information can be processed in one hemisphere and then communicated to the other through the corpus callosum. However, in these patients, the two hemispheres had lost their connection. They now could act independently, creating an incredibly unique opportunity for the research.

This sharing of information allows people to see an object with the left eye, process this image in the right brain and then share the information with the left brain, which can then produce words to communicate what they have seen externally. This is because the corpus callosum acts like a telephone line to send intel from one hemisphere to its counterpart on the other, ensuring both sides are on the same page. However, the patients with a split-brain scenario — where this phone line's been cut — respond slightly differently.

They can speak about things they see with their right eye that are processed by the verbal left brain, but can't verbally describe an object seen by their left eye, the domain of the right brain. If Sperry and Gazzaniga covered the patients' left eye, the visual information only entered their right hemisphere and this can't produce the necessary language to respond. While it would usually send a signal across to the left hemisphere, where the language would be processed, the corpus callosotomy stopped this. Patients would be lost for words, unable to say what they were seeing. Sometimes they replied that they could see nothing at all.

This is where it gets even more intriguing. Split-brain patients couldn't say what they saw, but were still able to identify what they saw by pointing or grabbing a similar item with their left hand (of which the right brain has full control). They were able to draw an object with their left hand, sometimes in great detail, but were not able to utter a word to name it. There is a real disconnect between what is being experienced and what can be described using different systems in the brain due to the functions of these different regions.

An interesting outcome of this is confabulation: a fancy word for a type of unintentional deception whereby one uses imaginary experiences or made-up information to fill missing gaps of memory. This is something many people experience. We add details or leave out some information due to memory distortion or imagination filling spaces of uncertainty. This was very apparent in the split-brain patients.

In one scenario, researchers wanted to see how a patient could follow written instructions shown only to their left eye. For example, they would visually present an instruction on a card for the patient to get out of their seat and walk around the table. The card was only shown to the left eye, leaving the left hemisphere of the brain clueless. Once the patient acted on the written command, the researchers interjected by asking them a question: 'Why'd you do that?'

Here's where it gets interesting. The left brain doesn't know why they got up. The right eye was covered and it wasn't able to access this information. However, like Mark Twain said, never let the truth get in the way of a good story. The storytelling left brain makes up a story to justify the action. They would commonly say something like, 'Ah, I just felt like stretching my legs'. Classic case of the left hemisphere crafting a story to justify an action it actually knew nothing about. This knack for whipping up explanations on the fly, even without all the facts, showcases the brain's incredible ability to fill in the blanks and paint a seamless picture of our actions and decisions.

This aligned with the work of psychologist Leon Festinger on cognitive dissonance. When our brain faces the scenario where reality doesn't line up with our beliefs or expectations, it throws us into a state of mental stress, creating an uncomfortable feeling called dissonance. The waters are muddied and we enter a mild state of confusion. Even this small level of uncertainty is something the brain doesn't like. Uncertainty is dangerous: the brain feels out of control and wants to rebuild certainty.

To smooth things over and get back in the driver's seat, our minds get creative, crafting reasons for why things happened the way they did, even if these reasons are not entirely factual. In the case above, the patient's left brain could have thought that their actions were random and not directed by their conscious self. That's when the dissonance would kick in. The left brain, not liking this one bit, started concocting a story to justify the action and reduce the implied randomness. But of course, this doesn't just happen to split-brain patients; we all suffer from this confabulation from time to time.

This natural human phenomenon to overcome cognitive dissonance is called 'post-decision rationalisation'. It's like looking back at what we've done and saying, 'Yeah, I meant to do that', even if we didn't intend to at all. We retroactively put a spin on our choices and actions, trying to make us look and feel a little more in control than is actually the case. Take the staunch supporter who justifies their favourite politicians' indiscretions as unlucky coincidences rather than their poor judgement. The person who buys an overpriced pair of sunglasses explaining they have superior quality, not just a flashy brand. Justifying the purchase of fast food due to being in a hurry, not the fact that it tastes so good. Many of us are very good at creating a story that reduces the dissonance and makes us feel better.

Which brings us back to the challenge of empathy: if we don't always really know why we do what we do, how can others? Think of a situation where you choose to do something. If someone asked you why you made this choice, is your answer actually the reason? Maybe it is, or maybe you are just creating an answer to reduce your own cognitive dissonance. This is yet another reason empathy can be so difficult and why it is probably the most challenging and important skill for people to develop.

Nice idea, but we're too busy

I've had a few disappointing days in my 20-plus years of working in large corporations, but one of the most frustrating of them all happened in early 2017. I was running the charitable foundation of a large insurance company. In the role, I reported to the group executive responsible for people and culture, meaning that among my peers were a collection of highly experienced experts in human resources, training and development. So, it was somewhat surprising when I was asked to conduct a project of research and discovery into how we could build empathy as a capability within the 10 000-odd employees across the organisation.

From my work with some of Australia's largest not-for-profit organisations, I had developed a deep interest in the power of empathy as a leadership capability and had suggested it was something we needed to build and develop across our people to enhance the business. When I raised this topic with my colleagues, I expected it to be either dismissed, or at best handed over to one of the learning teams to conduct research. Instead, the group executive suggested that if I believed in it, I should do it.

I spent many weeks deep diving into the world of empathy. I read leading books on the topic, reviewed the academic literature and devoured many hours of videos of people describing what empathy was and what it was not. From the brilliant mind of Brené Brown, the clinical experiences of Gabor Maté, Daniel Goleman's work on emotional intelligence and Paul Ekman's study of facial expressions, there were plenty of discussions on the importance of greater empathy in our modern world. Despite the mountains of great work, three things stood out to me as challenges for an organisation like ours in embedding empathy as a capability within such a large number of employees.

First, there were limited ways to measure individual or group empathy. While there are a number of tools used to measure an individual's empathy, many of these, like the Interpersonal Reactivity Index (IRI) and Toronto Empathy Questionnaire are self-reported surveys and not designed for large corporate applications. There are few objective measures and while close observation in clinical settings can be highly effective, they are impossible to efficiently scale across a large workforce.

Second, there were many nuanced definitions of empathy. As I touched on earlier, there are formal variations for affective empathy, cognitive empathy, compassionate empathy, somatic empathy, moral empathy and even global empathy. Each of these definitions has different targets of understanding and is aligned with different responses in the person displaying this type of empathy. While this creates a brilliant sandpit for academics to define their research and debate, it makes it difficult and confusing for non-academics to have a good sense of what is meant when people say, *You need to display more empathy*. Does this mean I should feel what they are feeling (affective), display these emotions myself (somatic), be compelled to do something about their situation (compassionate) or just understand their perspective without necessarily sharing that state emotionally (cognitive).

Third, I couldn't find a clear process that could be followed to build empathy. I knew from my many years in corporate life that if you wanted to impact behavioural change at scale across an organisation the size of ours, you needed to make the steps to change fairly simple and contained in number. While many of the experts rightly focused on building the skills for empathy, such as active listening, emotional awareness and perspective-taking, none had developed this into a systematic process that could be rolled out across hundreds, if not thousands, of people with any level of consistency.

Without the academic research budget required to progress with the measurement side of things, I dug deep into the development of a practical definition for our organisation and a simple-to-understand process for empathy. A definition I thought was both important and straightforward. I knew from my own experiences and internal research that any definition of empathy that would call on people to have a somatic response was not going to work. I could just envisage the challenges in asking hardcore finance people to display fragility in their body language to mirror a peer. Not only would it be unlikely, but also probably unhelpful. So, I used the simplified definition mentioned earlier that is most closely related to cognitive empathy: *understanding why people do what they do.*

Within a large organisation, this definition has the dual benefit that it can be applied across any stakeholder group. We want to understand why customers are buying or not buying. Why employees were working hard yesterday but not as much today. Why peers are making certain decisions we might not agree with or why people we report to might be doing the same. This definition of empathy is simple in meaning, easy to understand and most importantly has a clear utility for the organisation. If I can understand why someone is doing what they are doing, it can be useful information in building relationships, making decisions and taking action.

With the process, my intention was to provide steps that even the most analytically minded folk, like me, could follow. I also wanted it to be practical rather than just theoretical in nature. It needed to start where they were, in terms of their own thoughts, and help them to not only understand others, but support them in making decisions and taking action. I wanted to design the Empathy Process.

What I found was a number of nice frameworks that seemed to cover a lot of interesting points, but didn't really help with practical steps on how to build empathy. For example, I found seven keys of empathy:

1. eye contact

2. muscles of facial expression

3. posture

4. affect

5. tone of voice

6. hearing the whole person

7. your response.

While it is clever because it makes an acronym — EMPATHY — the idea of trying to train an actuary to monitor muscular facial expressions was not likely to work (sorry to any actuaries incredibly sensitive to facial expressions and not just staring into a spreadsheet). I was looking for a more structured process that had a clear starting point people could use to begin practising empathy.

After a considerable search, I decided the only thing to do was design and develop one from scratch. I spent many weeks working through different prototypes, developing multistep models, cross referencing the literature to ensure it made sense and refining through discussions with peers, experts and anyone else I could find. I became obsessed with creating a simple, easy-to-use model.

After a lot of draft versions, I finally landed on my Empathy Process. This four-stage process, which much of this book is devoted to, was something I was both proud of and confident could be used to develop empathy for people in our organisation in a reliable way. I took this process to my peers on the people and culture leadership team, feeling excited that I had developed something useful. They had asked me to go away and find an approach that would work and I felt this was very close to success, but sadly I didn't get the response I was hoping for.

While not in exact words, the response I received when I tried to discuss my Empathy Process was: *Nice idea, but we're too busy right now.* I'm certainly not the first person to have their work dismissed, but I was so invested in the process and the impact I felt it could have that it landed like a punch in the stomach. After a few meetings and conversations it became clear that while people in the team thought developing empathy sounded like a good idea, they didn't see it as a priority. I felt all my hard work was wasted and more than this, that the opportunity to really make a significant step-change in our organisation was lost.

Through disappointment came opportunity. While this company didn't prioritise empathy, I was more passionate than ever that this was a critical business skill all organisational leaders and professionals needed to master and that I had something useful to offer. With the support of my incredible wife Miranda, we decided to start Empathic Consulting. Our objective was to create a company focused on building empathy within organisations. The plan was underdeveloped and the road ahead uncertain, but I knew that there were people like me in organisations across the world who wanted to be more empathic and just needed help on how to do it.

Later that year, just weeks after Zoe's birth, I quit my comfortable job with the large corporation and started working out what building a consulting practice would look like. The journey of spreading empathy had begun.

CHAPTER 2

The Empathy Process: a step-by-step guide

The Empathy Process is straightforward, involving four major steps:

1. Being consciously curious

2. Openly exploring

3. Challenging your mental model

4. Leading with empathy.

Each step, as illustrated in figure 2.1 (overleaf), is crucial, and I will explore them in detail in this book.

Of all the steps, though, I believe the first one is possibly the most difficult and the final one the most important for modern leaders. In the pages of this book, we will journey through each step and explore the challenges we must overcome to build empathy. While the process is simple to look at, it can be complicated and exhausting to implement consistently due to the fast pace and diversity of modern workplaces. While it does take work,

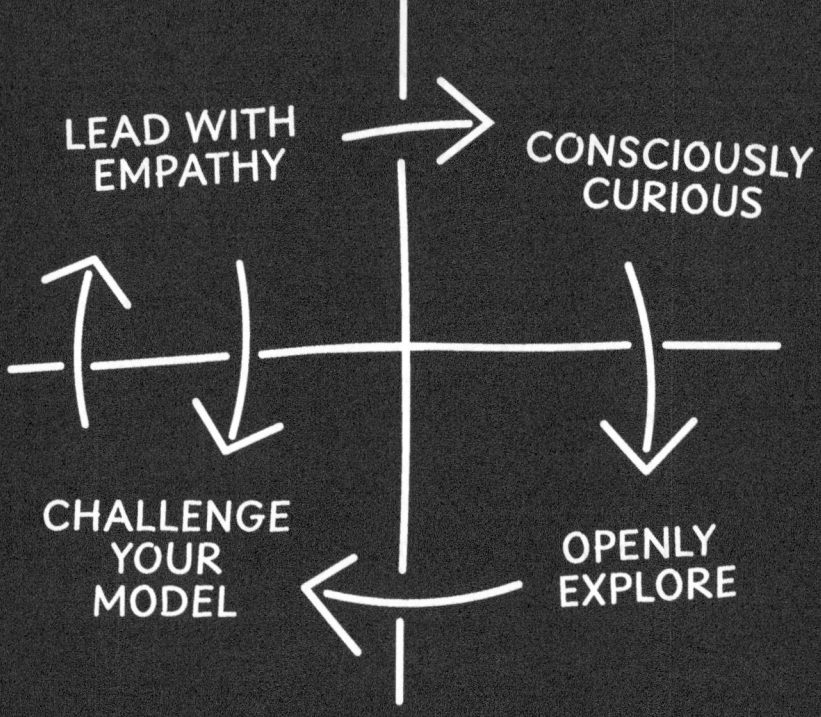

Figure 2.1: The Empathy Process

the benefits can be exceptional. Being able to understand what drives people, what they care about and the essence of their soul provides a foundation for incredible influence and change. Let's get cracking!

Assuming makes an 'ass' out of 'u' and 'me'

If you have never been to Mumbai, you should go. It's an incredible place. During my MBA study, we had the opportunity to travel to Mumbai to study some of the elements that made doing business in India unique. We spoke with the incredibly resilient and passionate management team of the Taj Mahal Palace hotel. World renowned for its exceptional levels of luxury service, the hotel was the site where, just a few years earlier, terrorist organisation Lashkar-e-Taiba had attacked killing 31 people, many of whom were employees. We visited the 250-year-old Bombay Stock Exchange (aka BSE), a world-class facility boasting some of the world's best trading speeds and where billions of dollars of trades are completed daily. We spoke with cultural experts, strategic leaders and CEOs from an array of India's largest organisations.

Our hotel on the trip was the luxury Hotel Sahara Star and it exceeded all my wildest expectations. From the outside, this large building appeared as a broad, grey cylindrical building with a large dome on its roof. As my taxi pulled into the driveway, I was nervous as to the conditions inside, but this quickly turned to excitement as the doors revealed glimpses into the inner paradise at the heart of the building.

Leaving the dusty, busy streets, with their constant noise and metallic-tasting air, the hotel is a tropical oasis inside. Luscious gardens spilling over terraces, the interior is full of vibrant green and smells of floral aromas mixed with delicate spices wafting from the kitchens. The roof is one of the largest pillarless domes in the world, covering the central, tropical lagoon. The plush rooms each have a sunlit private balcony to relax and work on looking down over this magical paradise.

While I had seen some people on the streets in Mumbai from the windows of the taxi, I had not really seen more than the corporate side of the city. One of my peers suggested we take a day tour to experience a different side of the city. She had found a local guide who offered walking tours of Dharavi, the biggest slum in Mumbai and one of the largest slums in the world. I was equal parts curious and nervous to venture into such a place, unsure if it was safe enough for a group of tourists. Just the word 'slum' conjured up a host of concerning ideas that made me think it might be a bad idea. Thankfully, curiosity won.

The evening before, we went to a local shopping centre. There I bought 50 packets of short, coloured drawing pencils. My thinking was that in Dharavi we would be approached by a lot of children begging. We had seen this on the streets and I expected it to be considerably more intense in the slums. I figured if a child came to beg for money, I could give them the pencils instead and they could use them to turn their dreams into colourful drawings.

The next morning when our guide came to the hotel to pick us up, I felt rather clever with my large bag of coloured pencils in my backpack. We began the drive to Dharavi and I shared with our guide my plan about handing pencils to the begging kids. His response: 'No. Do not give them pencils'.

I stared at him surprised and confused. He continued: 'No children in the slums will beg for anything from you. There are no beggars in Dharavi. Street people beg, not slum people. People who live in

Dharavi are proud, hard-working people and want nothing but to create a life for their families. They live here because homes in Mumbai are so expensive. This is the only place they can afford. But they don't beg'. His tone was one of defensive resolve and a touch of offence.

'If children come home with coloured pencils and tell their parents they came from a foreigner, the parents may think they have been begging and the children will be in trouble. No child will ask you for anything. Don't hand them out, please.'

I immediately felt terrible. Here I was thinking I was being thoughtful and compassionate when I was actually totally missing the mark. My actions were not of gracious charity, they were the often-experienced actions of another arrogant foreigner likely to cause more problems than they solve. Despite my own humble upbringing as a poor kid, I knew nothing about the people who live in Dharavi. I knew nothing about their world. Even after my visit, I still have little more than a slight glimpse into the lives of the million people who inhabit this twisted maze of lanes and makeshift homes in the middle of Mumbai. There are nearly a million people who call this place home and each of them is beautiful, unique and worthy of empathy, not my arrogance.

Instead of being curious, I had made a host of incorrect assumptions and jumped to conclusions. I assumed that kids would want coloured pencils because other children I had met had liked them. I had expected children would beg because I had seen people begging on the streets of Mumbai all week. I expected the parents of these kids would be grateful for the gifts I looked to share. I had no idea, but this didn't stop me filling the void of knowledge and cluelessness with assumptions. I assumed and I was wrong.

Assuming is something that is both completely natural, very common and predictably flawed. Many people know that making assumptions can be dangerous, so why do we continue to do it so frequently? The reason is simple: it is efficient. When you walk up a set of stairs, you assume they will not collapse, turning into some sort of fairground slide sending you hurtling to the ground below. How often do you test each step before you walk? When you pour coffee into a mug, you assume there are no holes that will cause the coffee to leak over the table. How often do you check the mug beforehand? We assume other motorists will stop at the red light as we turn across in front of them at busy intersections. Just imagine how much worse traffic would be if everyone waited on a green light just in case. Sometimes, these types of assumptions are convenient, useful and correct; other times they fail us badly.

Assumptions are beliefs or ideas that we accept as true without requiring much in the way of empirical evidence, making them easy shortcuts to understand situations and make decisions. They form a critical part of our cognitive toolkit, allowing us to navigate complex social and physical environments quickly and efficiently. Assumptions often fill gaps in our knowledge, helping us make decisions and respond to situations with incomplete information. We regularly rely on simple assumptions until we collect enough data to create more robust mental models. However, our brain struggles to distinguish between simple assumptions and well-backed factual models. This insight on how our brains actually work is important. We don't really know many things; we just build mental models based on our experiences and knowledge, which we use trustingly until we encounter new information that compels us to update them.

Mental models are internal representations our brains use to understand the world around us, predict outcomes and guide our interactions. These models are constructed from past experiences, education, cultural norms and many other forms of learning. Few are innate but many are learned very early in our lives. Between birth and age five, our brains are incredibly malleable, quickly creating models for language, motor skills and basic social-emotional navigation. These models simplify the overwhelming complexity of the real world by providing a framework through which information is rapidly filtered, interpreted and acted upon. Within three months of being born, human brains are already able to differentiate between faces expressing happiness, sadness and anger. By age two they can begin to understand how expressions are linked to emotional states and events that can cause them.

However, the speed and efficiency provided by assumptions and mental models comes with a downside. While they allow for quick decision making and reduce cognitive load, they can also result in types of errors, biases and misconceptions that lead to thinking we are right and being completely wrong. Exhibit A: my bag of coloured pencils. While this caused me some embarrassment, little damage was done. However, these assumptions and misinterpretations can also be much more serious.

In 1999, Amadou Diallo, a 23-year-old Guinean immigrant living in New York City was standing outside his apartment building when he was approached by four police officers. The police were following up leads on a serial rapist in the area and thought Diallo fit the description. The officers ordered Diallo to raise his hands, but, startled and confused, he instead reached into his pocket to retrieve his wallet. The officers mistook this confusion and motion for aggression and reaching for a weapon. Within seconds, the officers had discharged 41 rounds from their guns killing Diallo, who was both unarmed and had no criminal record.

In some cultures, particularly in Asia, maintaining eye contact with authority figures is considered disrespectful. However, in Western cultures, it is often interpreted as a sign of attentiveness. If a doctor, unaware of these cultural differences, maintains constant eye contact while discussing the patient's condition, the patient might feel uncomfortable and perceive the provider as arrogant or aggressive. This misinterpretation can reduce trust and compromise the quality of care the patient receives.

In courtrooms, judges and juries often assess the credibility and trustworthiness of defendants and witnesses based on their demeanour. This has become most prevalent in asylum seeker cases in the United States where the stress of recounting traumatic experiences can cause otherwise deserving asylum seekers to come across as deceitful or evasive. Different people develop different mental models to deal with certain types of situations. But when shame causes a person to look away or hasten their speech, it is easy to understand that another person with a vastly different perspective can see this as something else.

The good news is that because assumptions and mental models are simply ideas in our heads, we can change them. Mental models can and should be updated and evolve with new information, experiences and learning. The process of revising our mental models to accommodate new data is a crucial skill. This flexibility and learning requires self-awareness, analysis, the ability to challenge ourselves and the humility to admit we are wrong. As vital as these are, they take time and often a lot more cognitive effort than making assumptions.

The real problem is not in making assumptions or relying on mental models. It is in our ability to discern when they might be wrong, the awareness to then stop relying on them blindly, and to conduct more detailed conscious analysis. So, why don't we do this more often? Why can't we more easily control our thoughts?

The rider's illusion of control

The human brain is an extraordinary piece of biological equipment, capable of processing vast amounts of information from our environment. Every second, it's estimated that the brain receives approximately 11 million bits of data. This information is flooding in from so many different places. Our visual, auditory and olfactory systems give us information about the world around us. Senses of touch, pressure, temperature, taste and other systems monitor the interaction of our bodies with our more immediate environment. Internally, our brain is sent information from all the internal organs including the internal neural chatter. The brain is constantly flooded with an incredible stream of data on the internal and external worlds, which is used to make decisions on actions and processes that must be taken.

Most of this data, though, is consciously ignored. Despite the amazing computational power of our conscious brain, it can't even get close to processing the deluge of data we receive. The conscious brain, responsible for our experience of awareness, deliberate thoughts and intentioned actions, has a very limited processing capacity. Psychologist Mihaly Csikszentmihalyi, author of the highly influential 1990 book *Flow: The psychology of optimal experience* stated that the conscious mind can only handle 40 to 50 bits of information per second. That's about 0.0005 per cent of the total available data. While there is a flood pouring through the gates, only tiny droplets are being processed by your conscious mind. The remainder seem to pass by, largely ignored by your conscious thought, but not lost entirely.

This great processing gap highlights an essential aspect of human cognition: the vast majority of the information our brains process happens outside of our conscious awareness. While it is nearly impossible to measure exactly how much is processed by the subconscious, our best guess is a massive amount.

This underappreciated part of your brain is constantly analysing, filtering and directing attention to what is deemed most relevant based on past experiences, predicted needs, emotional responses and biological priorities. It uses assumptions and mental models to instigate actions, responses and thoughts based on the data constantly flooding in.

We don't, and simply can't, consciously be aware of every minute detail inside and around us every moment of our lives. While we can sometimes consciously control our breathing, it is primarily outside of conscious control. It takes great effort to overcome hyperventilation and if you've even seen an athlete being interviewed right after an event, you will have seen the wrestle the conscious brain has to try and halt their rampant panting to be able to speak.

We don't have conscious control over thousands of biological processes and systems that keep us alive. Instead, our brains use various automatic mechanisms to decide which pieces of information to manage immediately, which to ignore and which to bring into conscious awareness. For example, when we are walking up a large set of steps, our subconscious brain receives messages from the muscles in our legs, demanding more blood flow. Our heart is instructed to beat faster, capillaries to dilate and, responding to an increase in core body temperature, sweat glands are instructed to excrete salty water from our skin to cause evaporation, cooling the blood that has been pushed into blood vessels closer to the surface. Muscles increase their consumption of adenosine triphosphate, causing the breakdown of glucose and spurring the need for greater production of this energy source by the body's mitochondria. The complexity of these processes is unbelievable and the sensitivity and adaptability of the human body is truly remarkable.

Imagine the strain, though, if we had to consciously think through and engage all of these processes just to walk up a set of stairs? We digest food, fight diseases, dilate our pupils to adjust to light conditions, repair damage, alter blood flow and pressure...It is a constant state of action and reaction that is generally out of our awareness, let alone our control. If survival counted on my conscious mind processes, I'd be dead in seconds. I can't even remember to take the reusable shopping bags when I go to the supermarket. Imagine if I had to remember to keep my heart beating!

While we might think it fine for many of those homeostatic processes that keep us ticking to be managed by the subconscious, surely the important decisions are dealt with in a more calculative and strategic way full of nuanced considerations, right? That would certainly make us feel a little more in control. Sadly, modern research shows this is simply not true.

Psychologist Jonathan Haidt uses an ancient Buddhist metaphor to elegantly describe the relationship between the conscious and subconscious brains. Imagine an elephant with a small man riding on its back. The rider is your conscious brain, with all its incredible complexity of thought, computation, self-control and rationality. The rider provides humans with our complex language and communication skills, ability to develop and share complex information, and conduct long-term strategic planning and forecasting like no other animal on the planet. The rider is amazing and generally the rider thinks they are in full control of the person.

The elephant in this metaphor is your subconscious brain. As we have seen, the subconscious actually takes care of almost all the things that keep you alive. But it also heavily influences more seemingly conscious action. The rider may think they are in control, but when the elephant is angry and wants to charge, we find out just how little control the rider has. If you have ever said something in anger you regret, made a decision that in hindsight you thought was impulsive and wrong or gone with your gut instead of your head, then you have felt the power of the elephant.

Road rage is an all-too-common example of the elephant taking over. Let's say someone named Bill is driving his car when another driver rudely cuts in front of him causing him to brake sharply. What happens next? Does Bill:

- make a calculation of the amount of additional time he has been inconvenienced on his travel before responding to the other driver based on this quantum of impact?

- react impulsively with anger and frustration at the rudeness of the other driver, who did something they were not meant to do, beeping his horn furiously and waving his arm out the window?

From my experience, Bill most commonly chooses the latter. The actions of the other driver cause a pulse of surprise and fear in Bill. He reacts instinctively by hitting the brakes to avoid an accident. Then, despite the immediate danger being avoided, an emotionally charged elephant takes over and Bill is filled with anger. This other driver, seemingly the one who caused this surge of negative emotion, becomes the target of our angry elephant and these emotions fuel the beeping, arm waving and associated responses that follow. They are not the responses of a conscious rider; they are the outburst of a cranky elephant.

Studies by Australian insurance company Budget Direct found that 80 per cent of people surveyed felt angry or annoyed when others drove dangerously and 83 per cent reported having been shouted at, sworn at or on the receiving end of rude hand gestures made by other road users. This was consistent for people surveyed across all ages, genders and professions. According to the UK *This is money* website, one UK national poll even found that doctors were the most aggressive drivers. Although this was a self-reported survey, this may imply the stress and pressure of their jobs puts their elephants on edge, or indicate that doctors are also the most honest when reporting their behaviour behind the wheel. It should be noted that when surveyed, almost 80 per cent of people say they are better than average drivers — let that statistical impossibility sink in before we trust too many self-reported road studies results.

Road rage is a common example of what happens when the elephant's impulsive reaction takes over, but it is certainly not the only one. When the elephant is triggered, it can make us do things well outside the boundaries of what we would consider logical or sensible. Shakespeare understood the elephant well. When Romeo finds Juliet's lifeless body and is so overwhelmed with grief that he takes his own life. When Juliet wakes to find Romeo dead, she follows him to the grave. The lovers are often described as tragically romantic and impulsive, but like many of his masterful pieces, Shakespeare captures the nature of the elephant perfectly.

The elephant's emotional responses and reliance on mental shortcuts can push us to many irrational actions and behaviours. Scary movies rely on your elephant taking in the images and sounds from the screen to ignite a set of mental models in your brain and having it trigger a sense of fear. *Nightmare on Elm Street* would be pretty dull if you couldn't find Freddy scary due to your conscious brain simply rationalising that there is no danger given that Freddy is just an actor wearing makeup and can't possibly hurt you. When you think about it, we should never get scared of movies. We know they are fictional yet many of us still look away or cover our eyes due to fear, both of which are responses ironically unhelpful in the face of any material danger.

Inside us all live a rider and an elephant. A capacity for deliberate, calculated and rational thoughts alongside a powerful instinctive and intuitive core, driven by assumptions, emotions and simple mental models that are capable of taking over at any given moment. Maybe, like some of the 80 per cent of people who think they are better than average at driving, you think you have your elephant under control and this description of irrationally instinctive people is only about others. If this is you, maybe ask people close to you. I've found many people convinced they are purely rational; however, when I ask their partner or a close friend, they are very prepared to give them a reality check.

Being consciously curious

The year 1984 almost didn't happen: 26 September 1983 was almost the last day for humanity. As the commanding officer of the Oko nuclear early-warning system, the Soviet Air Defence Forces' Lieutenant Colonel Stanislav Petrov had the fate of the world in his hands. It was the depths of the Cold War and tensions between the United States and the Soviets were at an all-time high. For many years, the United States and NATO had been pressuring the USSR with deployments of weapons and military activities that meant many in the Soviet Union felt an actual attack was imminent.

Bruce G Blair, former president of the World Security Institute, described the Soviets as being on 'hair-trigger alert'. Just two years earlier, the Soviet military had shot down a Korean Air Lines flight, killing 269 passengers including a US congressman. It was a time when both sides had the means, and seemingly the intent, to destroy the other if they felt they were being attacked.

As the great scientist Carl Sagan described it: 'The nuclear arms race is like two sworn enemies standing waist deep in gasoline, one with three matches, the other with five'.

It was expected that any strike by the United States would be immediately countered by the USSR, ensuring they were able to counter attack with their own nuclear arsenal before US missiles made impact. While this would lead to mutually assured destruction, the only fate worse would be the possibility of an unanswered attack leaving the Soviets decimated and without the means to retaliate. It would take close to half an hour for any nuclear missile launched by the United States to hit Soviet targets — plenty of time to enact their planned protocol: the immediate launch of a counterstrike of nuclear weapons aimed at the United States ensuring there would be no winners in this war.

Just after midnight on 26 September, alarms sounded at the Serpukhov-15 bunker just outside Moscow. This facility was home to the USSR's best defence, a state-of-the-art Oko early-warning capability. The alarms were triggered when the satellite detection system identified that the United States had launched a surprise attack. It was from known nuclear missile silos and it was likely headed towards Soviet targets. As the officer on duty, it was Lieutenant Colonel Petrov's duty to report this to his superiors immediately, an act that would set off a well-understood, yet terrifying chain of events: instant retaliation in the form of a full-scale Soviet launch which would see hundreds of nuclear warheads, already aimed at US targets, launched.

The US Congress has estimated a Soviet nuclear attack would kill between 136 million and 288 million people. Possibly billions more would perish from the nuclear winter that would follow, leading to starvation in a post-apocalyptic nightmare. The eyes of everyone in the room turned to Lieutenant Colonel Petrov, expecting him to pick up the phone and inform his superiors, although many likely dreaded the consequences. But Petrov did not pick up the phone. In a moment of calm curiosity in the eye of a nuclear storm, Petrov didn't simply follow the orders blindly in a panicked reaction. He paused and thought about the situation carefully, considering not only the information from the warning system, but also the broader situation and the nature of the enemy they faced in this bitter cold war.

As he described the situation: 'My cozy armchair [in the bunker] felt like a red-hot frying pan and my legs went limp. I felt like I couldn't even stand up'. The pressure was incredible. However, Petrov knew that any pre-emptive US action would likely be a full-scale attack. He expected in this situation they would launch hundreds of nuclear missiles simultaneously, hopefully gaining the element of surprise, and cause as much destruction as possible with this single assault. But the Oko early-warning system indicated that only a small number of missiles had been launched. Why so few?

The clock continued to tick. Everyone in the room looked at Petrov and at their watches, counting down the minutes until possible impact. Why had he not picked up the phone? Still, Petrov thought, Ground radar had not identified any incoming missiles and no additional missile launches had been detected. This didn't add up for the lieutenant colonel. If the United States was really attacking, why only a few, isolated missiles? He knew there was one more possibility: it could be a false alarm.

As the time ticked away in the building tension, Petrov became convinced that this was indeed the case. He didn't pick up the phone and alert his superiors to the alarm. Subsequently, no Soviet retaliation was ordered. Millions of people around the world slept comfortably in their beds, oblivious to the fact that they had been so very close to never waking up. The countdown to impact ran down and there was indeed no impact; there had been no pre-emptive US strike. Petrov breathed a deep sigh of relief.

In this moment of intense pressure, Lieutenant Colonel Stanislav Petrov saved the world through one of the most powerful actions any leader can take: being consciously curious. Curiosity in the face of intense pressure and strict orders is a skill we must practise ourselves and embed in our leaders and teams. The complexity of our modern world provides too many opportunities for outdated assumptions, innocuous errors, rigid mental models and strict rules to create situations of disaster.

The ability to pause, especially when the clock is ticking as loudly as it must have been in Stanislav Petrov's ears, is the skill we need to develop and practise to have greater empathy. This is conscious curiosity: the ability to momentarily pause existing mental models and assumptions and view a situation without judgement; to be a blank canvas of interest, openness and curiosity. In this state, we fully recognise and admit that we already hold assumptions, but we don't allow these mental models to automatically guide our beliefs, thoughts or actions. When a situation arises where we need to have more empathy, the first thing we must do is pause and actively park our existing mental models — let go of them at this moment, becoming unencumbered by our existing beliefs.

The reason this active suppression of our existing mental models is important is not only to allow free space for new information to flood in, but because without parking our models our brains do something even more damaging than assumptions alone. We can fall into an all-too-common, and sometimes very useful, strategy for processing information in a complex world. Instead of seeking information, we seek validation.

The brain is hungry for certainty

In the twisted web of the human mind, where logic and emotion often wrestle for control, a subtle yet powerful tendency seems to emerge. This tendency, known as confirmation bias, represents our innate preference to seek, interpret and recall information that validates pre-existing beliefs, rather than spending cognitive energy and precious time exploring new ideas. This inclination not only shapes our perception of the world but also profoundly influences our decision-making and problem-solving capabilities.

Confirmation bias isn't merely a quirk of human nature but a fundamental aspect of how our brains function. As discussed earlier, we are constantly bombarded by almost ten trillion bits of data every day, day after day. This data is overwhelming but within this mass of information are the critical pieces we need to put together for survival. The brain's major function in the world is to trawl through this deluge and find those pieces that really matter. Inevitably, the brain will encounter times where it comes across information that conflicts with previous ideas or information currently being processed. The pieces don't match and we suffer cognitive dissonance. This holding of two or more contradictory beliefs, ideas or values at the same time causes brain distress. Which to believe? Which to ignore?

Confirmation bias isn't merely a quirk of human nature but a fundamental aspect of how our brains function.

A simple example of this dissonance is motion sickness. As a lover of boats, I have regularly taken people into the ocean who have consequently fallen ill. But what causes this onset of violent vomiting? On a moving boat, your inner ear detects the motion of waves rocking you up and down, forward and back. However, if your eyes are focused looking inside the boat — for example, looking at a person, screen or table that is also rocking and rolling with the waves — your eyes don't detect any motion. Relative to the boat, you are still. This results in the brain receiving two conflicting sensory signals, moving from the ears but still from the eyes, which causes cognitive dissonance.

Triggered by this type of dissonance, our brain evokes an ancient defensive tactic: vomit. One of the main ways we can influence our bodies is through ingestion of substances. We have all probably felt queasy after eating something that wasn't quite right and this feeling could mean we have ingested some sort of poison. When we suffer this sort of dissonance, our brain responds by emptying the contents of the stomach in the hope of ridding the offending substance. Some people do the same before a big exam, on a date or before a public speech. The dissonance of fear, excitement and concentration create a sea of conflicting signals in our minds, so the elephant takes over just in case it was something we ate.

Ultimately, brains have evolved to deal with this tsunami of information not by processing all of it with careful scrutiny, but by looking to simplify it with processes and mental models to reduce levels of dissonance. As psychologist Beau Lotto describes in his brilliant book *Deviate: The science of seeing differently*, 'Uncertainty is the problem that our brains evolved to solve. Resolving uncertainty is a unifying principle across biology, and thus is the inherent task of evolution, development, and learning'.

Generally, it is much easier, safer and efficient to fit the pieces of data into an existing model than to attempt to create new models constantly on the fly. This psychological default reduces dissonance and preserves our psychological comfort. As the old saying goes, 'Better the devil you know'. For thousands of years, the ability to make rapid judgements based on limited information meant the difference between life and death. Today, these shortcuts still remain important for navigating life, but they also mean we too often seek out information that confirms our preconceptions, overlooking evidence to the contrary, and sometimes fail to truly understand the complexities of the modern world. This in-built need for comfort comes with a cost, too often leading our brains to seek comfort in assumptions rather than objective truths. These shortcuts, assumptions and biases also inhibit our capacity for empathy, understanding and critical thinking.

The implications of confirmation bias aren't just limited to individuals; it can also be a team sport. In social interactions, it underpins the echo chambers and filter bubbles that characterise modern social and political debate. Any followers of US politics would see the reinforcing ideas propagated from both sides through media channels such as Fox News and MSNBC. When MSNBC was touting the validity and importance of mask mandates during the pandemic, Fox News was fuelling scepticism. While Fox News propagated messages of tampering in the 2020 election loss of Trump, MSNBC focused only on the importance of the democratic process. For MSNBC, the rise of the Black Lives Matter movement was an overdue focus on the deeply embedded, systemic racism across the country. However, for Fox News, the same movement was a chaotic and lawless uprising inspired by Marxism and a sign of the breakdown of law and order within the country. Which side was right? It is almost a pointless question. What is more impactful is what channel you regularly watch. This polarisation is an ancient phenomenon that has become increasingly easy to see in the internet age. We find the people, messages and ideologies we agree with, build on the preconceived ideas and rally with fellow believers to strengthen the voice of the cause. We follow those who agree and scorn those who do not.

Search engines and social media algorithms, which are designed to help us navigate through the noisy internet and find things we are looking for, further reinforce our existing beliefs by predominantly presenting us with content that aligns with our previous choices. If you read more Fox News articles, it will show you more similarly related articles and fewer from the opposing side. If we support left-wing spokespeople, we will see more comments from aligned media mouthpieces. This constant feedback loop exacerbates the divide between differing perspectives, making it increasingly difficult for us to engage in any form of open-minded discussion.

Combatting confirmation bias requires a conscious effort. We must break the natural inclination to seek fast conclusions and instead swim in the uncertainty of curiosity. This mindset of exploration sounds fun, enticing and adventurous, but it is also more dangerous. Curiosity killed the cat, after all. Conscious curiosity involves actively seeking out diverse perspectives, subjecting our own beliefs to critical scrutiny and being willing to accept the uncomfortable dissonance that may result.

While this bias for confirmation is a deeply ingrained aspect of the human mind, our awareness of this can also pave the way for a more flexible, open-minded and, ultimately, more accurate understanding of the world. Without challenging the ideas of the past, we would never have the brilliant technologies of the future. We must challenge our predispositions and embrace the complexity of differing ideas. We can and must become curious about the more nuanced and complex perspectives that are being constantly formed and propagated around us.

In the Soviet bunker, Petrov's conscious curiosity saved billions of lives, if not the survival of the human race. The ensuing Soviet investigations into the incident found that the Oko nuclear early-warning system had detected the sun's reflections on clouds over a nuclear missile silo site and mistaken it for a launch. Harmless reflections almost caused the end of life on the planet. What is so ironic is that the very technology that had been developed to improve human decision making fell victim to the same mistake so many humans fall into: it collected data, made an assumption of the meaning and reacted by suggesting an action that was completely inappropriate given the reality of the situation.

Fortunately for all of us, on that day a curious leader, Lieutenant Colonel Stanislav Petrov did not simply react to the data. Petrov was more open and flexible in the mental models he used to make sense of the data. He embraced his uncertainty and in the face of incredible pressure utilised the powerful skill of empathy for his enemy to save us all. Today, we have more technology than ever before to provide us with data and, while it is constantly improving, it too will require us to remain curious before acting haphazardly. I can only imagine what life might be like today if Petrov had been feeling overly tired, stressed or upset. Would he have made the same decision? Who knows. What would you have done in the face of this incredible pressure?

In May 2017, Stanislav Petrov passed away at the age of 77. He never thought of himself as a hero, just a man who was doing his job. However, I think we should all take a moment on 26 September each year to reflect on the actions of this humble lieutenant colonel and be grateful for his calm, conscious curiosity, without which, the world would be a very different place.

CHAPTER 3
Navigating uncertainty with empathy

In October of 2019, news broke that the Australian government, led by Prime Minister Scott Morrison, had spent almost $200 000 hiring an empathy consultant to provide advice. No, it wasn't me but, as you might imagine, the media took great pleasure in the aftermath scorning the apparent admission of the leader of our country being so out of touch with his constituents that they needed someone to help them to have empathy. Also unsurprisingly, as the CEO of a company called Empathic Consulting, I had media agencies reaching out for my thoughts on the matter.

In a live radio interview, they asked me an obvious question: 'Did I think politicians needed to have more empathy?' My response might not have been exactly what they were expecting. I responded that I thought politicians actually have a lot of empathy...for other politicians. In most political situations, if you don't have a good understanding of the motivations, desires and beliefs of the other politicians you need to work with and against, you won't have much success in the job. Successful politicians are typically masters at navigating the complex web of competing priorities across the house of parliament. They tap into the needs of other members of the house and use this knowledge to build influence, create leverage and ultimately help them in reaching the outcomes they desire.

'What I think you are asking is whether politicians need more empathy for everyday people,' I said to the reporter. 'I just think it is hard because what does an everyday person look like?'

My reply probably wasn't the tasty, Morrison-bashing soundbite they were after. But then again, I'm not sure their question was really asked with the intention of doing much more than confirm their existing belief. Media interviews generally are conducted in this way. The media outlet has a direction it wants the conversation to take, so the reporters ask very specific questions that look to put the interviewee in a certain position. Most often, it is looking to either trumpet a position they see as favourable or to squeeze someone into discomfort when they don't.

A perfect example of this, and a humorous one in my view, was in 2020 when, on Sky News, UK Health Secretary Matt Hancock was being asked about the appointment of former Australian Prime Minister Tony Abbott to be a UK trade ambassador. Mr Abbot had a rather interesting reputation based on his time in Australian politics including some views that were considered quite offensive in parts of society. The interviewer in this instance, Kay Burley, phrased her opening question on the matter like this:

'He [Mr Abbott] says he feels threatened by homosexuality. He also says elderly people should have been left to die naturally from COVID-19 and men are better set to exercise authority than women. Is he the right sort of person to represent us?'

In the vision from the interview, the health secretary is clearly wearing an NHS Pride flag badge on his jacket and with the introduction to her question being such a scathing indictment of Mr Abbott, you might think that it should have been an easy answer for Mr Hancock. What happened next wasn't the finest few minutes for Mr Hancock, but I suspect it was exactly what Sky News was hoping for from the question.

First, Mr Hancock dismissively admitted he didn't agree with Mr Abbott's views on homosexuality but emphasised that the United Kingdom needed Mr Abbott's experience and expertise. Unsatisfied with his attempt at brushing aside the criticism, Ms Burley pressed further on her opening comment regarding Mr Abbott's views.

Mr Hancock tried to declare that he didn't think this was true, but Ms Burley didn't let it go, forcefully repeating her points, making sure they landed clearly.

It was at this point that Mr Hancock, probably feeling conflicted and in a bind, really dropped the ball and fell into Burley's trap. He replied, 'Well, he is also an expert in trade'.

Check mate. At this moment, Hancock had attempted to make a point he probably thought was poignant about Mr Abbott's credentials for the particular role. However, under the pressure of time and the attacking style of questioning, he blurted out these words he no doubt regretted very soon after. In reality, this was probably the soundbite Sky News was dreaming of when it planned the interview. Burley had laid the trap and Hancock just walked right in. The suggestion from Mr Hancock was that the government was willing to overlook the uncaring, homophobic and misogynistic behaviour of a person appointed to a critical position as long as they were enough of an expert. Expertise trumps intolerance. If you have the skills, you can get away with saying reprehensible things. This was a train wreck.

But let's also be honest about the motives behind the interview — Ms Burley's questions weren't really questions. She knew that

Mr Hancock would support the decision his government had made in appointing Tony Abbott to the role. He had to tow the party line. She also knew that Mr Hancock was an advocate for LGBTQIA+ rights, having supported same-sex marriage and spoken out in favour of LGBTQIA+ equality in healthcare. Ms Burley knew that by asking her questions the way she did, it would make it almost impossible for Mr Hancock to support the decision of appointing Mr Abbott without sounding hypocritical. It wasn't really an exploratory interview — it was a trap.

The sad reality in our modern world is that this is an all-too-familiar type of discourse that many people would witness on any given day. On news channels around the world, guests are invited with the intention of asking them tricky questions looking to catch them out. As a species, we are the most sophisticated communicators on the planet, but we are also likely the most sinister. In discussions, people too often look to score points rather than seek understanding.

The combative nature of many political and intellectual discourses often fosters an environment of strategic warfare rather than the thoughtful exploration of ideas. Conversations morph into battlegrounds, where questions are not bridges to understanding but traps laid with cunning precision. Such environments reflect broader social trends of echo chambers and filter bubbles seen in social media, where confirmation bias reigns supreme. It seems many people see themselves today as leaders rallying their army around some momentary conviction with the aim of beating down any dissenting voices.

The digital era, with its algorithms and echo chambers, has certainly accelerated this divisive tendency. Online environments are carefully designed to stimulate emotional responses, shape our experiences and support our existing preferences. These spaces help entrench existing beliefs and widen the chasm between our own and conflicting viewpoints. We are drawn into ideological conflict and rewarded with support in the form of comments and likes from those who agree with us, spiking our confidence in our position.

While it is common for us to see this behaviour in the 'other side' we don't often enough acknowledge that we are too vulnerable to a descent into ideological skirmishes where curious exploration might be more appropriate. From social media 'likes', online forums that upvote content and even the late-night comedians who mock right-wing politicians to the rapturous applause of largely left-wing audiences. Sure, it might feel fun as the dopamine hits, but are we really getting anywhere useful? Are we learning and growing our understanding?

To navigate beyond this battlefield of ideas, a shift towards curiosity and exploration is critical for personal and societal growth. This demands active and sincere engagement with conflicting perspectives, a willingness to ask open questions and a genuine desire to seek to understand. We must be more comfortable in questioning our own beliefs, and have the courage to confront the unknown.

This journey from confirmation to curiosity can't just be an intellectual exercise that other people probably should do. To practise empathy, we must lead and do this ourselves. We must ask questions that help build a more nuanced and multifaceted clarity of our world. While the act of conscious curiosity prepares us mentally for the opportunity to openly explore, it won't happen if we are simply drawn back into the cut and thrust of idea protectionism. We can break free from the confines of the unknown, but it won't be a spectator sport. We must enter the arena. To embark on a more open-minded exploration of the ideas that shape our world, we are going to have to find better ways to disagree.

To navigate beyond this battlefield of ideas, a shift towards curiosity and exploration is critical for personal and societal growth.

Disagreeing without being disagreeable

Given the combative environment we are surrounded by, it's not surprising that many of us have problems navigating the complex terrain of disagreement without succumbing to disagreeableness. Constructive disagreement requires an approach that values the person behind the perspective and seeks to more deeply understand their viewpoint without trying to disprove their ideas, defend your beliefs or damage the relationship between you both. This can be quite a delicate endeavour, where clear intentions and constant awareness are needed to not step over the line. This needs not only the intellectual smarts to explore the topic but also the emotional intelligence to explore, understand and even challenge with empathy and respect.

To create an environment where disagreement for the sake of understanding can flourish, we must champion the second step in the Empathy Process, the principle of openly exploring. This involves creating an environment where different perspectives can not only exist, but are welcomed with open arms. This is a space where the strength of an argument is measured not by its volume or ferocity but by its interest and validity for further thought. The squeaky wheel shouldn't always get the oil; instead all ideas are considered and allowed to exist. It needs us to have a commitment to curiosity and a willingness to explore the unknown of another's mind.

Due to the combative nature we often experience in modern conversations, our response to someone challenging us too often involves several predictable steps.

First, activation in the amygdala, the emotional core of our brain and a core part of the elephant's domain. The amygdala is highly sensitive to threats in our environment and can process this information even before we are consciously aware of it. This rapid detection mechanism enables quick responses to potential dangers, even when they are not particularly real. When a disagreement triggers the amygdala, our elephant can launch into fight-or-flight mode, shutting down other processes in the body and brain, enhancing memory formation to focus on what is already known and reducing the capacity for curiosity.

Often in conjunction, this firing within the amygdala can coincide with activation of the hypothalamic-pituitary-adrenal (HPA) axis. These three areas of the brain interact closely in response to stress with the release of cortisol and adrenaline. Our blood pressure and heart rate increase, our focus is enhanced and glucose levels are increased. This is the elephant preparing for battle. In this state, our cognitive capacity can also become constrained. With chemicals flooding our brain to increase focus and response speed, our ability to remain calm and explorative are heavily diminished. The rider is partially blinded as the elephant stampedes towards safety.

To disagree more effectively, we need to be sensitive to the way comments impact our elephants and cautious about the influence they have on our response. When you hear an idea you don't agree with, be aware of how it makes you feel. Do you feel your heart rate increase, a pulse of emotion or a sense of frustration? These can all be signs that your elephant has been stirred. Don't panic. Be curious about these reactions and sit with them. See this as a sign of something interesting being uncovered. Your elephant isn't wrong, it has just encountered something different and we must learn to not let its initial reaction turn into more than is useful.

This is part of a broader process called emotional self-regulation, allowing us to influence and manage emotions and how they are expressed. This capability is important to much of everyday life. Improving emotional self-regulation can improve personal relationships, workplace performance and our own mental health. This taming of the elephant involves having the ability to tolerate uncomfortable emotions without them taking over. We can then modulate our emotional response to appropriately match the situation.

In her brilliant book *How Emotions Are Made,* Lisa Feldman Barrett describes how emotions are not universal, automatic responses to stimuli but rather are constructed in our minds through processes that involve memory, situational context and sometimes irrelevant information from the environment. For example, if I told you we were entering a haunted house with a creaking door and the wind whistling through a window, this might create a totally different reaction than if I told you we were entering a summer beach house. The fear response in the former situation is not due to the noises alone — there are other factors at play. When we are feeling tired, the difference between disappointment, frustration and anger can be difficult to distinguish. The response we might have if we misinterpret disappointment as anger can be inappropriate and not useful. It is convenient to look for an external excuse for our poor response: *You made me upset; that's why I reacted that way.* The reality is, it is within our power and responsibility to own our emotional responses and we must improve at controlling them.

Emotional awareness starts with acceptance: acknowledging that feelings happen without any excess labelling or judgement. We then need to deploy strategies to manage and alter the intensity of emotions to align with the situation and what we are trying to achieve. Sometimes, this might be as simple as taking a few deep breaths and other times it will involve more deep thought and perspective-taking exercises (which we will explore in more detail below). Ultimately, the goal is to not let the elephant take over. We want the rider to be more in control as we navigate the complex world of different opinions and reduce the likelihood of impulsive reactions that might lead to outcomes we regret.

An important element of emotional self-regulation is the differentiation between adaptive and maladaptive strategies. Adaptive strategies tend to lead to better long-term outcomes. An adaptive strategy in the face of conflict might be to use humour to reduce tension in a conversation, whereas maladaptive strategies tend to provide a temporary sense of relief with more damaging long-term consequences. A great example of this was Russell Crowe's response when BBC's Mark Lawson asked a question about the actor's accent for the character Robin Hood. Lawson began by suggesting that Crowe's famous English character had hints of Irish in his accent, to which Crowe replied, 'You've got dead ears mate. You've seriously got dead ears if you think that's an Irish accent'.

Lawson tried to backpedal by emphasising the words 'hints of' but this did little to subdue the clearly irritated Crowe.

'Bollocks…I'm a little dumbfounded you could possibly find any Irish in that character. That's kind of ridiculous.'

Lawson tried again to regain the civility in the conversation by confirming it was an accent from northern England but at this stage it was too late. What followed was Crowe sarcastically suggesting it was actually an Italian accent he was going for before abruptly ending the interview by walking out.

Whether you think the actor's reaction was justified or not depends on your interpretation of the accent he uses in the movie, a debate I won't weigh in on here. The reality, though, is that this combative response was completely ineffective at capturing more data or information regarding Lawson's perspective. It is a classic example of an aggressive, maladaptive response to threat whereby at the end of the exchange, Crowe may have felt justified in his response. However, it likely didn't do much to improve his reputation as a friendly person to interview in media circles.

The ability to self-regulate emotions is not easy. Practices such as mindfulness meditation have been shown to enhance emotional awareness and acceptance. Similarly, psychotherapy and counselling offer strategies for people struggling in this capacity too. You will need to find the best way to regulate your own emotions and if, as for many others, it is a challenge for you, don't despair. While empathy and understanding others is challenging because it involves the complexities of another human, emotional self-regulation is all about you. It is totally within yourself to manage this more effectively and I believe it might be one of the greatest investments you can make. Being able to control your emotions is vital to remaining consciously curious.

The journey towards mastering the art of disagreement is a testament to our ability to sit within our own discomfort and uncertainty. To manage any threat responses our brains might have and explore the areas of disagreement as opportunities for new knowledge rather than points of division. Listening to differing views opens the door for more ideas to be found. Embracing nuance paves the way for greater nuance to exist. In a world of such complexity as our own, this is what we need to explore further: the places we don't agree with. For this to work, we need to reinvigorate the art of asking questions and seeking to understand.

Using the right questions for empathy

My grandmother, Beryl Murray — or Nana, as I always called her — was an incredibly compassionate and kind person. My daughter Zoe was only five years old when she passed away and despite only spending meaningful time with her on a few occasions, my daughter was very upset when she died. Nana's funeral was not too long after our family dog, Misha, had passed away and Zoe was trying to reconcile these events in her young mind. We encouraged her to ask lots of questions to help her work through the events.

One day, we had the following conversation:

'Dad, is Nana dead?' Zoe asked.

'Yes Zozo, Nana died,' I replied in a sombre voice.

'And Misha is dead too, right Dad?' she pressed.

'Yes, darling, both Misha and Nana are no longer alive,' I replied.

Zoe looked away for a few moments, then turned her face to me and asked, 'Dad. Before I was born, was I dead?'

This question floored me! I had no idea how to answer. While I hadn't really thought about it too much, my mental model was that people were either *alive* or *dead*. As somewhat of an atheist, I had at times considered and reflected on what happens after people died and explored the likes of the afterlife and Heaven, but never had I thought about before birth. Was she alive before? If she wasn't alive, was she dead? If she wasn't dead or alive, what was she?

Once I moved past my initial shock at not knowing a useful answer, I began to reflect on and deeply admire what Zoe had just done. She had become curious enough, in a subject matter that can be emotionally difficult to discuss, to ask a question that helped us both explore new territory. These are the types of questions that create fresh space in a world crowded full of information. The type of thought that opens the door to innovation. It didn't claim to have an answer, it simply took an existing mental model and enquired about an element she wanted to explore further.

When empathy is the aim, these are often the ultimate types of questions. However, they don't necessarily need to always be this deep or thought provoking. When considering different types of questions, the categories in table 3.1 can be helpful in determining the types of questions we ask and the outcomes we seek.

Table 3.1: types of questions and the outcomes they seek

Question type	Description	Example
Contemplative	Explores areas outside of the current known space and encourages others to investigate the unknown	*What would you do next if you knew you were going to die in 90 days?*
Exploratory	Deepens understanding of the current areas or underlying drivers of existing knowledge	*What do you really love about your current work?*
Navigational	Used to create a map of the known territory and helps to group and categorise through complexity	*What are the main tasks you complete in your daily role?*
Closed	Usually Yes/No questions aimed at confirming information already known or thought by the asker	*Do you like going to work each day?*
Loaded	Most commonly statements disguised as questions designed for strengthening one's own position	*You don't like working in this horrible place every day, do you?*

The types of questions that Kay Burley asked Mr Hancock would be considered in the categories of Closed and Loaded. The first — 'Is he the right sort of person to represent us?' — sought only a yes or no answer, although it also followed a very loaded and unflattering description of Mr Abbott making a 'yes' answer almost impossible. Her second question — 'Even if he is a homophobic misogynist?' — was less of a genuine question and more of a loaded statement to push Mr Hancock into a bind. These aren't questions asked with the intention of understanding or empathy.

These types of questions are commonly used in modern battles we disguise as discourse. There are many examples of people with this aggressive, attack-style interviewing. Some of the more prominent ones are Allan Jones here in Australia, Piers Morgan in the United Kingdom and Tucker Carlson, who was allegedly fired for being too aggressive even for Fox News, in the United States. Some might think of these people as bullies, and I'd not be inclined to defend their journalistic integrity, but I think we need to realise that their job is not to wade through the uncertainty and uncover the complex wisdom and truth beneath. They are confrontational in nature and provide little opportunity for genuine conversation to follow. Their job is to cause controversy, capture attention and sell advertising. They are no more attempting to engage in curious discovery than WWE wrestlers are engaged in legitimate competition. We need more. We deserve more.

If we consider the Venn diagram in figure 3.1:

- Area 1: There is information we already know inside the Us bubble,

- Area 2: In the Them bubble exists information known by the other person,

- Area 3: There is of course information known by Us and Them,

- Area 4: Then there is information that sits outside known by either Us or Them.

Loaded questions are generally used to confirm and strengthen the information inside area 1. They are used to confirm what is already known by Us. We use Loaded questions in an attempt to reinforce our own position and gain advantage within the conflict. Loaded questions typically try to highlight what is within our existing knowledge to the other person to urge them to agree. We don't learn much about the actual topic from

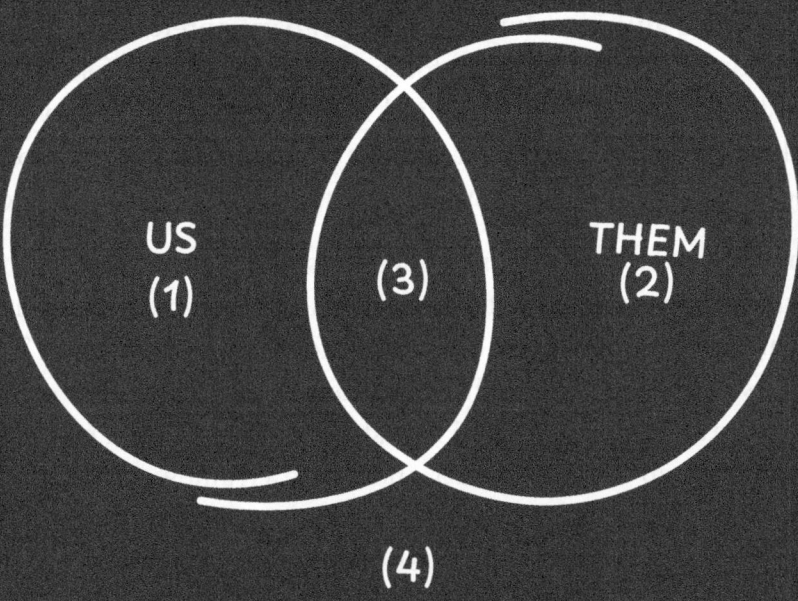

Figure 3.1: Us and Them

Loaded questions, but they can certainly help us understand the opinions and feelings of *Them*. Loaded questions are perfect for antagonising, insulting and annoying other people, but that is well outside the pursuit of empathy.

Closed questions can be used in this way also. We ask questions designed to confirm or what is already in the field of Us. There are times when they can provide a small amount of information within area 2, but the level of granularity is typically low. If I were to ask, 'Do you like cheesecake?' I would expect either a yes or no answer that gives me a limited insight into your preferences. Closed questions can also be used for gaining permission for further questions, such as, 'Do you mind if I ask you about your work?' While the answer might not provide a lot of useful information, it does build the trust and confidence for further questions to follow.

This is where navigational questions can be used to provide a greater level of insight from which to explore; for example, 'What sort of activities do you perform in your work?' This allows for a grouping of information to be set out that can be used to further explore and investigate. Navigational questions provide a map of areas 2 and 3, and create a framework for deeper insight and information to be structured around. Without useful navigational questions, the vast expanse of ideas that could be investigated in trying to establish empathy and understanding can be overwhelming.

If I want to understand more about *Them*, it is more effective for me to choose a specific area within area 2 to begin the empathic journey rather than trying to understand the incredibly vast complexity of the person all at once. For all people, the landscape of information that could be explored will be massive. We are all full of stories, nuances and intricacies that form up who we are. It is useful to survey and map out a part of this before diving into Exploratory questions. Good Navigational questions provide us with a set of high-level sign posts to delve into and can be used to ensure the exploration is both useful for your purposes and welcomed by the other person. This is not to say other aspects of the person we are looking to have empathy for are less important, but having a complete understanding of someone is a mammoth task. Navigational questions can help us to focus and help the other person have a clearer understanding of the types of topics you might be interested in understanding.

This is a critical element of openly exploring. We must be aware that while we want to explore to build empathy, that doesn't mean the other person will want to share this information with us. Creating a space where individuals feel safe to be seen and heard is important in enhancing the effectiveness of communication and understanding on a deeper level.

Permission is a cornerstone of empathic interactions. It signals respect for the other person's boundaries and willingness to engage in what can be sensitive conversations. By first seeking permission, we acknowledge the autonomy and comfort level of the other person, which is more conducive to open and meaningful dialogue. Asking for permission also demonstrates emotional intelligence and sensitivity to what might be going on for the other person. Not everyone has time or energy to answer a series of questions, and at times this can be a very unwelcome burden. While we may be ready to dive into deep exploratory questions, the other person might not be in the right frame of mind. This awareness and respect for the other's emotional and mental space can significantly impact their willingness to share.

With permission, we can have a more impactful exploration, even on subjects that may be challenging or uncomfortable. We want to ensure that diving into deeper questions will be a shared and congenial journey, marked by mutual understanding and respect, rather than an intrusive or overwhelming experience.

Once we have useful reference points and clear permission to continue, we can now use the navigational points identified as areas to dive deeper with Exploratory questions. This requires us to engage in our Conscious Curiosity, park our existing beliefs and genuinely explore area 2, the world that is known to them but not yet known to us.

The art of exploration

Starting with foundations of conscious curiosity and an environment of trust allows for greater exploration and understanding to occur. However, to build the skills of empathy we need also to be able to ask good exploratory questions that help to uncover the information that will provide greater insight. This is why exploratory questions are most often open-ended and crafted to create the opportunity for the other person to provide more information.

Exploratory questions play a pivotal role in building empathy, serving as essential tools for unlocking deeper insights and fostering ongoing, meaningful dialogue. These questions should invite the other person to delve into their thoughts, experiences, beliefs and emotions. Conversations become richer explorations of topics, going beyond the highlights and waypoints provided by the Navigational questions and diving into the underlying essence of the person.

By encouraging others to share their perspectives, Exploratory questions facilitate an exchange more focused on them than us. We want to ensure the person we are empathising with is the centre of the conversation and avoid making this a mission to find what we are looking for. When done well, both parties will experience a richer conversation. Combative questions invite the opponent to fire back, like a tennis match where each is trying to beat the other through their loaded questions and protective responses. When we are exploring openly, questions serve as an invitation for the other person to provide answers that open a door for a world of discovery. The other person can express nuanced viewpoints, share personal anecdotes and offer unique perspectives. This approach not only fosters a sense of empowerment and engagement for them but also facilitates a more holistic understanding of complex topics for us.

We can further enhance the experience for the other person we look to empathise with through active listening and displays of curiosity. Active listening is a fairly simple practice but, in my experience, rarely completed well. At the heart of active listening is paying full attention to the other person. In our modern world, this is becoming increasingly challenging for many people.

A dear friend of mine, John, always wears a nice analogue watch. I hadn't thought much about it other than as a fashion accessory until we had dinner one night. I wear a smartwatch connected to my phone that vibrates on my wrist any time my phone has a notification. I'd estimate that about 90 per cent of the time, the notification is neither urgent, nor important to attend to immediately, but as John pointed out to me, that doesn't stop me checking my watch every time it vibrates. Do you have the same routine? Some app on my phone is triggered to provide a notification, my watch vibrates and I look at it to see what it is. John then told me, that is the reason he wears analogue watches. When he is speaking with someone, he is fully engaged. He turns his phone ring and vibrate off and puts it away in a bag or pocket so he can be fully present. I now do the same when spending time with people, except I also take off my watch.

One sure-fire way to break the connection needed for empathy in a conversation is to be constantly distracted by something else. For some people it is the watch or a mobile phone; for others it might be a television or a child they are being distracted by. No matter what the other subject of your attention is, every time you point that attention away from the person you are talking with towards that other target, you break the connection. Full attention is vital.

This is rarely more important than when speaking with people through a virtual video call. COVID-19 spurred an incredible surge in the use of video conferencing applications such as Zoom, Teams and WebEx. While video conferencing is inferior to in-person conversations, it provides greater richness of experience than email or phone conversations alone. However, due to the relative lack of experience many of us have with this technology, we are not all that skilled in using it effectively. All too often, I have observed participants on video conferencing calls with eyes moving as they read something on their screens that is clearly not related to the speaker. I see people typing away or looking at a second screen, head turned to the side as someone talks.

If this is you, I understand. The temptations are so large. There is a universe of other things you can explore. The whole internet is at your fingertips — likely there is also a list of emails and other items demanding your attention. However, every moment you fail to pay full attention is noticed. In particular, the person speaking will notice. That window you project through the video is being closely monitored by everyone else on the call. They will be watching carefully at the attentiveness of your eyes and gestures. If you are not paying attention, it will be noticed and have an impact. Focus is required: pay full attention, particularly on video conferences.

Another critical skill in openly exploring might be the simplest in theory yet seemingly difficult in practice. In 2013, after many years of speculation, professional road racing cyclist Lance Armstrong sat across from Oprah Winfrey. Despite being there essentially to confess, Lance continued to initially dodge and deflect in his answers. However, Oprah cleverly used the magic of strategic pauses and silences after posing probing questions to allow Lance the opportunity to contemplate and consider his responses further. In a memorable instance, Oprah asked Lance directly if he had used banned substances to enhance his performance. After having denied the allegations for many years, Lance was now faced with Oprah's unwavering gaze. Her expectant silence left an emptiness in the conversation that required filling.

During these moments of silence, Lance visibly struggled with his internal conflict before eventually admitting to using performance-enhancing drugs throughout his cycling career. This use of silence created a tense and demanding atmosphere that prompted Lance to confront the truth. This led to a watershed moment in the interview that, while not totally surprising, was one many suspected would never occur. Lance Armstrong admitted to cheating in front of an audience of many millions.

Attentive silence is a powerful tool in the empathy toolkit. It creates a space that, generally in conversation, we look to fill. All too often, when we are looking to validate our ideas or have questions rigidly prepared, we fill the space with a question to serve ourselves. Instead, let the silence be an invitation to the other person. Allow the space for their initial comments to sit with them and an opportunity for expansion upon them. When we move on too quickly or jump into our next question, we can cut off deep insight that is mere seconds away.

You can also take this to another level by listening to the person with wonder. One of the great pleasures of being a father is seeing wonder in my daughter's eyes. When I've read her a book she loved, or told her a fun story, she looks at me with big saucer eyes and it is like the rest of the world just fades away. For that moment, we are bound in a pocket of time all of our own. They are magical moments of connection.

I don't believe it is my storytelling or the book itself that creates this magic though. It is the attention and wonder from my little girl that makes it so special. We should all try to listen like this when we are speaking to people we want to understand. Lean in. Hang off their every word. Be deeply interested in their answers and display your intrigue in your body language. What I don't mean is to gain interest in the hope of winning them over. That is disingenuous and will likely come across as patronising. Instead, actually be fascinated. Practise the art of blocking out the rest of the world and create a moment in time of deep connection. You will be amazed at just how fascinating other people are when you listen deeply with conscious curiosity.

One of the most simple, yet powerful, ways to demonstrate curiosity and active listening is to follow an initial answer with the response, 'That's interesting; tell me more about that'.

This is a particularly useful phrase to use when you are exploring a topic that may be contentious or one you are in disagreement with. For example, imagine I wanted to have more empathy for someone who believed the Earth is flat. This belief had been generally agreed as false by scientific minds for many hundreds of years. However, now it is a view held by an estimated 17 million Americans and many others around the world — yes, around the world (it's ironic, I know). In any exploration of this topic, I would be likely to hear perspectives and ideas that do not align with my own. Instead of either disagreeing openly and entering a debate, or pretending to agree with the person and being inauthentic, this sentence provides an opportunity to encourage further discussion without bringing conflicting beliefs into the conversation.

This is a critical element of open exploration — it is not the place for challenge or debate. It is all about uncovering and investigating their world. Avoid interjecting or interrupting. Another useful technique when there is a lull in the conversation is to summarise and reflect back your understanding of what they have said. Here is a simple example of this being used by David Letterman when interviewing Malala Yousafzai, the Nobel Peace Prize laureate and education activist.

In their conversation, Letterman frequently paraphrased Malala's statements to ensure clarity and to delve deeper into her experiences and perspectives. During conversations regarding Malala's activism in the face of incredible challenges, Letterman paraphrased her journey:

'So, what I understand is that despite facing threats and danger, you continued to advocate for girls' education because you believed it was crucial for the future. Is that accurate?'

This technique helped Letterman to summarise Malala's courageous efforts and allowed her to provide additional insights into her motivations and beliefs. Notice it was posed as a summary to display understanding plus a question that opens the door for refinement. Throughout his many years as an interviewer, Letterman's use of summarising and paraphrasing built trust and understanding, and facilitated more insightful and engaging conversations with hundreds of interesting people.

The objective of openly exploring is to gather a rich set of information about the person you are looking to empathise with. In particular, we want to explore as much as possible about the person that is currently outside our knowledge and avoid the common trap of being fixated with validating our existing views. From figure 3.1, we want to explore area 2, the space that is known to them but outside our own knowledge. We want to increase our breadth of understanding and allow the two circles to overlap more than before.

At this stage, we have looked to capture new information about the person we are looking to empathise with. We have built a level of trust and asked open, exploratory questions. We have listened with conscious curiosity and demonstrated our attention through summarising and reflection. We have not necessarily agreed with their views, nor passed any judgement on their beliefs. We have simply sought to understand more than we did before about this amazing human. This idea of being fascinated by the other person underpins the first two steps in the Empathy Process: consciously curious and openly exploring. Now it is time to thoughtfully consider this information.

Exploring from a distance

The year 2020 was a strange one for most people around the world. Gripped by the COVID-19 pandemic, sickness and fear was widespread. Here in Australia, many people were feeling the additional impacts of movement restrictions, social distancing laws and heavily enforced lockdowns. This unique and peculiar situation saw people reacting in very unusual ways. Healthcare employees were under intense pressure, families were torn apart and conspiracy theorists had a field day with the uncertainty.

Amid this chaotic time, there was one behaviour I saw repeatedly being reported on the news that I thought was particularly strange. It was the great toilet-paper hoarding of 2020. Footage of shopping trolleys overflowing, people scrambling for the last pack of dunny rolls hiding at the back of otherwise empty shelves and store employees desperately trying to keep people calm. Some even resorted to violence. I remember seeing a video of three middle-aged women pulling at hair and throwing punches, all over a few cylinders of two-ply paper.

My initial train of thought when witnessing this behaviour was simple and judgemental: *This is madness.* I thought this was simply poor behaviour by people who were panicked about something they shouldn't have been concerned about. Silly people doing silly things. Maybe you thought something similar? Maybe you think I was being harsh? Maybe you participated in this action and have some other views on the matter? In reality, my initial judgement lacked empathy.

We all do this sometimes, don't we? As discussed in chapter 2, assumptions are our default and we use them quickly and efficiently to assess a situation and make judgements. While my assumption about these people being silly was quick, it wasn't particularly useful. What could I do with this point of view? If I wanted to influence a change of this behaviour, what approach would I have? Tell people:

'Hey, stupid person. Stop being silly'?

Do you think that would actually work? Probably not, right? If we want to influence people, particularly in a leadership position, it is critical that we seek to understand why people do what they do. I'm certain that if we were to ask people clambering over each other to reach the last roll, they wouldn't have said their motivation was lunacy. This type of judgement is fast and easy, but not very useful.

Empathy requires curiosity and exploration, but what if it isn't possible? In this case, spending time with the toilet paper warriors wasn't feasible and this is not an uncommon situation. There are many times when we may seek to have empathy but are unable to access the people needed to explore in person. This is where using a tool like the Perspective Taking Model can be helpful.

I designed this tool to be simple to remember, easy to use and flexible in application. The only objective of the tool is to help stimulate thoughts outside of our usual assumptions. It is not designed to give us the correct answer, but to get us to find many possibilities. Figure 3.2 (overleaf) illustrates the model in full.

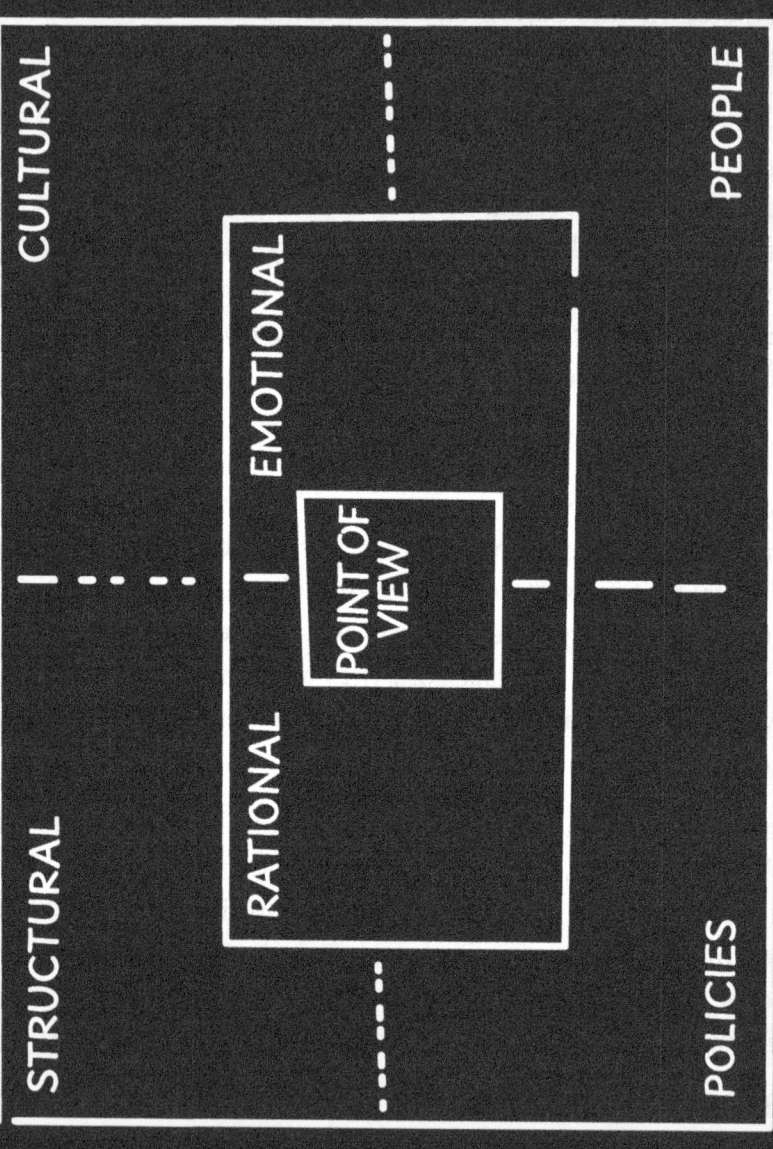

Figure 3.2: the Perspective Taking Model

The first step is to write in the small rectangle in the middle the perspective you are looking to understand. This will often be a perspective you don't agree with, something you don't understand or find significantly diverges from your view. For the scenario I described above, I might put 'Toilet-paper hoarding' into this box.

Next, I look to explore any rational reasons why someone might decide to hoard toilet paper and place these in the area labelled 'Rational'. These might include ideas such as:

- *they need toilet paper:* they feel it is a necessity worth fighting for

- *shelves are empty:* with limited supply it is justified to hoard

- *it's not reusable:* it's not like you can just use one piece for a few days to ration it out

- *I can't make my own:* well, you probably can, but it would be very coarse

- *I'm not going to stop needing it:* you can't try to hold everything in for a few weeks — that will turn out very nasty.

You might think these are not very compelling rational reasons, but this is not about convincing you. Your benchmark of 'rational enough' is irrelevant. This is about looking outside the perspectives you already hold and exploring divergent alternatives. Some of them you may partially agree with or even see as valid — if somewhat uncompelling — but that doesn't matter. Someone who performs the act of toilet-paper hoarding may see these as rational reasons and that is what we are looking to explore.

In the area marked 'Emotional' I would complete the same exercise thinking about the emotive drivers of this behaviour.

Again, don't use your emotional drivers as the benchmark, instead look broader:

- *Fear:* they are scared of missing out and not having enough

- *Embarrassment:* what would people say if they had none?

- *Greed:* they deserve it more than anyone else

- *Love:* they don't want their family to suffer the inconvenience of not having toilet paper

- *Justice:* there's an overwhelming sense of unfairness in them not having what is their right to have.

Again, you might see all of these as weak reasons, but this is not about you. You simply recognise that these could be emotional drivers for someone and may be data points worth considering. For the Structural and Policies areas, we are considering other tangible drivers at the macro and micro levels. For example, the fact there was a global pandemic and supply chains were being impacted globally may have been a factor in their decisions and actions. Also, at the localised level, there were purchase limitations being enforced and rapidly changing isolation laws that could have played an influential role.

On the right-hand side, we can explore the Cultural drivers that may influence their decisions. Culture is a big driver of behaviour and if we were living in a competitive and individualistic culture, it could certainly shape our behaviour to prioritise getting our own toilet paper over the concerns of others. Finally, other people have a huge impact on our beliefs. It might be family members, friends or even television personalities who influence the panic buying of toilet paper. This gives us a model that looks something like figure 3.3.

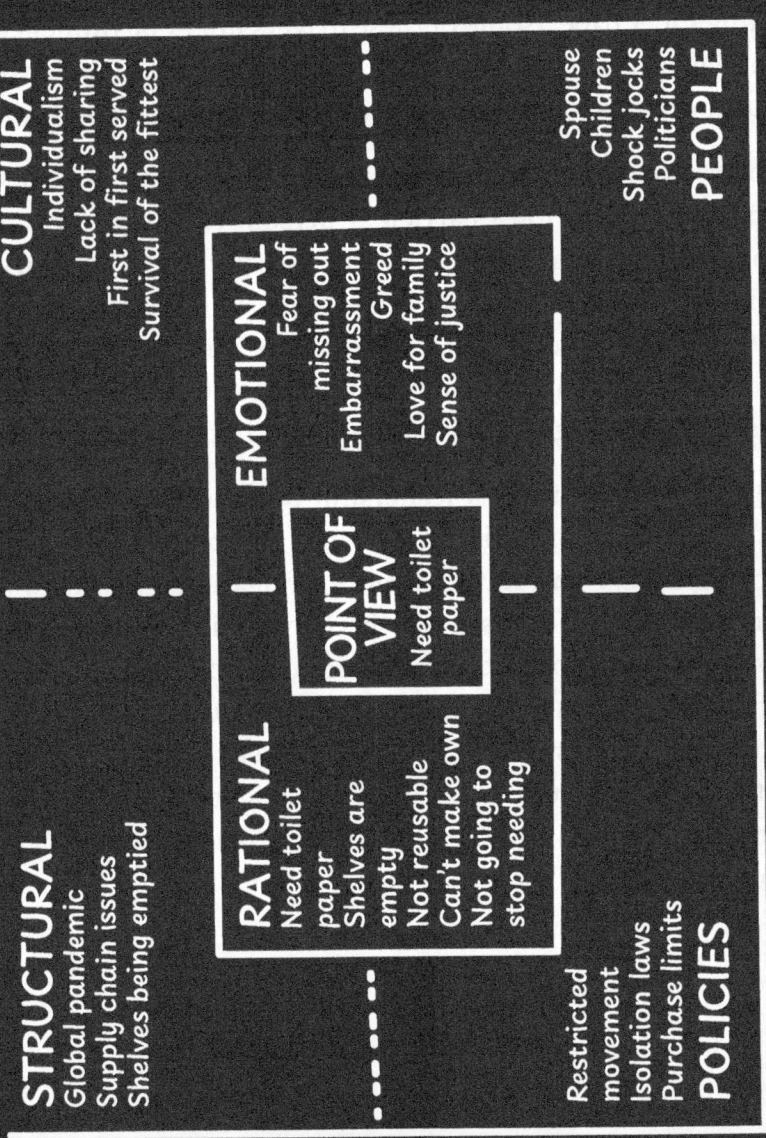

Figure 3.3: a Perspective Taking Model example

When stepping back and looking at this model now, there are a lot of reasons why someone might see hoarding toilet paper as justified in their circumstances. For any particular person who is hoarding toilet paper, some of these drivers might be influencing them. Maybe none of them are and instead there are more beyond my quick exploration at play. In some cases we will never know.

The objective of the Perspective Taking Model is not to land on the specific reasons for a particular person. Nor is it to change our own mind or to agree with the perspective. To clarify, I personally still see toilet paper hoarding as a misguided practice, but what I have done is created a range of new perspectives to consider. My rigid and instantaneous judgement has now been superseded by a range of possibilities I was initially blind to.

More importantly, from a leadership perspective, if I wanted to understand the specific drivers of a person who was toilet paper hoarding, I now have far more navigational marks to use for my questions. This is what the Perspective Taking Model really gives us: more starting points to explore individual beliefs. It doesn't give us answers and when using any of these points to begin questioning, I should be very comfortable with admitting that my guesses within the model may be completely wrong. But at least I now have many more places from which to explore openly.

CHAPTER 4

Challenging the way you see the world

Through spending time to openly explore with conscious curiosity, our objective is to collect information that we may not have had before. Sometimes this information will be structured, unambiguous and quantifiable. Other times this information will be messy, confusing and unverifiable. But it is information nonetheless.

One thing you may not yet know about me is that I love cycling. I love the feeling of freedom and exhilaration of leaning deep into corners, descending long hills and, maybe most of all, climbing steep mountains on a road bike. I'm obsessed with watching the Tour de France and will stay up all night during the race, in particular to watch the best cyclists in the world battle it out on the famous climbs. Any ascent of Alp d'Huez, Col du Glandon and Col d'Izoard are all among my favourite stages to watch. For years I had sat on my couch in the wee hours of the morning, watching the battle of the best and secretly dreaming of tackling them myself.

In 2016, my wife and I were in France as part of our long journey to become pregnant. We were travelling around staying in beautiful towns through the Alps and each time we reached a new town, I would hire a bike and find the best climbs nearby to test myself on. I had managed to tick off the three mentioned above. When we started our journey across the southern half of France towards Avignon I decided we needed to make a stop at a small town called Malaucène.

I went in to town in the afternoon, found a bike shop and hired the most beautiful Pinnerello bike I could find. The next morning, I would tackle the hardest of all the climbs on the trip: Mont Ventoux. Approaching from Bedoin, this climb is a famous and legendary challenge. This scenery is spectacular and the road tortuous. The mountain starts at the quaint village of Bedoin. From there, I started the 21.5-kilometre climb to the top. Yes, it's all uphill from there.

The ride actually begins gently with lush vineyards and oak forests, providing a deceptive comfort through the first few kilometres. Quickly, though, the road starts to ramp up in front of you. Once your legs are burning and lungs gasping for air, you hit the middle section. This is typified by long and unrelenting sections of road that average around 9 per cent in gradient and, for a bit of variety, spike even higher in parts.

Just when you think you might be close, the scenery shifts dramatically. The trees lining the road vanish and you enter the iconic barren moonscape of the upper reaches of Mt Ventoux. Without the trees, the wind starts to batter you and the sun seems to double in intensity. You think it must be only a few more pedal turns until you look up to see the final few kilometres of road. No more shade, shelter or respite and all uphill—this is the true test of resilience for even the most seasoned cyclists.

Finally reaching the summit, I looked down at my cycling computer. It had taken me just under two hours. I now sat with my bike at 1912 metres looking across the beautiful landscape of Provence. The views were breathtaking. From the Alps to the sea, this was my prize. I was met by my kind-hearted wife, who had driven up the other side of the mountain to greet me at the meteorological station. It was a moment I will never forget. A rite of passage for cyclists, conquered.

After this, my wife drove down and I started the hair-raising descent. Hitting speeds over 80 kilometres an hour, exhilaration swept through my tired legs as I gripped the brakes and swept through the sweeping bends. Despite a few scary moments, I made it back to our Airbnb safe and sound. While Miranda cracked a bottle of champagne, I hurriedly went to my laptop to upload my GPS data from the ride. As a middle-aged man in Lycra — affectionately known as a MAMAL — many of us like to upload our ride data to a website called Strava (see strava.com) to record and compare our ride against the 120 million other users of the site.

Once the upload was complete, I excitedly looked at the leaderboard for the epic climb. To my disappointment, my time was pretty unremarkable. I was within the top 30 per cent of people, but at nearly two hours, my time was nearly double the best recorded time on the site. My heartrate data was pretty average too. High, but nothing special. As I scanned on, I felt empty. The data was boring. I immediately thought, if people at the head offices of Strava were reviewing the data from Mt Ventoux, they'd look straight past my data. Nothing to see here.

The thing was, though, that boring was not my experience at all. This was the peak. This experience was as good as my cycling career would likely ever get. In my mind this was an epic battle of chubby little MAMAL against one of the most challenging sections of road on the planet. This was a two-hour story where I ended as the hero standing with my girl atop the summit of this beast of a mountain, but my devices hadn't captured this. Strava didn't record my experience, just my numbers. In doing so, it left the most critical information for me on the slopes of Mt Ventoux.

While this might not be of any significance to anyone but me, it does make me question the approach many organisations take in gathering data and making decisions. Using quantitative data is very important, but we must be cautious not to expect that the numbers tell the whole story. If you ask a parent how many children they have, this will give you an interesting number. If you ask them to describe the personalities of their children, the depth and richness of the information that follows will be far more profound. If you wanted to buy gifts to bring to give to their children for a celebration, which question would be more useful for you in choosing appropriate gifts?

Making data-driven decisions shouldn't mean only using numbers. It should be about gathering important, relevant and accurate information, then synthesising this information to create a useful foundation from which to strategically explore the options available and make the best decision to help move you towards your goals. While numeric data fits neatly into spreadsheets and calculations, it doesn't always capture the most important or most relevant information. When humans are involved, ignoring the subjective, psychological information such as emotions, opinions and beliefs is not only short-sighted, but can also be very costly.

A perfect example of this occurred in late 2020. During the global lockdowns caused by the COVID-19 pandemic, many businesses that relied on traditional, face-to-face retail were struggling to stay afloat. One such retailer, GameStop, was facing an existential crisis. The rise of digital downloads and streaming services had been steadily eroding its customer base. When the lockdowns compounded this, their formerly bustling stores seemed to be nothing more than deserted relics of a bygone era.

As the company's stock price languished, it became a prime target for hedge funds, which saw it as a fading star and wanted to profit off the decline like vultures circling a wounded beast.

Short selling is essentially betting against a stock. In this investment strategy, an investor borrows shares of a stock they believe will drop in value by a future date. After borrowing the shares, the investor sells them at the current market price. If the price falls, the investor can then buy back the shares at the lower price, return the borrowed shares to the lender and pocket the difference as profit. However, if the price of the shares increases, the short-seller will incur a loss, as they must buy back the shares at the higher price to cover their position. Based on the decline of similar bricks-and-mortar retailers such as Blockbuster, HMV and Borders, a number of hedge funds decided to bet on GameStop's demise.

Three in particular took very strong positions against the games retailer: Melvin Capital, Maplelane Capital and D1 Capital Partners. Using their analytical research, they determined that GameStop's decline was a sure thing. What data sources might they have not taken into account? Reddit, the massive group of online communities where people can cluster and discuss specific topics of interest. It is almost certain they ignored this information source for far too long.

The reaction of members of one group in particular, r/WallStreetBets on Reddit, to the idea of these big hedge funds trying to feed on the dying carcass of a store they actually liked was very strong. Discussing the short selling of the Wall Street elite, the community banded together to create a 'short squeeze'. Individuals from the community invested their hard-earned money in the stock, creating a shortage and forcing the hedge funds to buy back their shares at the now higher price. This, in turn, pushed up the price and realised further losses for the short-sellers.

Partly fuelled by a narrative of challenging the dominance of institutional investors and hedge funds, many investors started to see real gains in their investment value despite not fully understanding the risks involved or the underlying financial health of GameStop. The social media hype drove the stock to extreme highs, detached from the company's actual business fundamentals. By January 2021, the share price had soared from below $20 to a high of almost $500. Meanwhile, Melvin Capital, Maplelane Capital and D1 Capital Partners found themselves haemorrhaging billions. The stock's volatility was unprecedented, spurred on by rallying cries on social media to hold the line and not sell the shares. Actual figures are not publicly available; however, it is estimated it cost Melvin Capital in the order of $5 billion, Maplelane about $1.5 billion and D1 Capital Partners around $4 billion.

While the saga raised many valid questions about the role of social media and regulatory control in markets, it does highlight that despite the sophistication of investors in using data and algorithms to make decisions, ignoring the ability for groups of people to disrupt can be very, very costly. Humans are amazing creatures and while we sometimes behave logically, we have built the modern world of systems of beliefs, culture and connection, which are at times the most powerful and chaotic forces on the planet. As the world becomes more complex, we need to be more vigilant in our exploration of all relevant information to factor into our decisions.

Bringing a scientific mindset to beliefs

The GameStop saga was a good example of the way tribalism will be a force that continues to shape our world, maybe more than ever before. Tribalism is engrained deep within us. We like to back our team, support our side and defend our turf.

We are particularly defensive of our tribe when we think we are under attack from outsiders. While these attacks were historically physical in nature, more often today we see the attack as a challenge of our ideas. *They* are trying to suggest *we* are wrong — how dare they!

In the world of the internet and social media, even distant groups are hyperconnected. This hyperconnectivity creates both the opportunity for physically distant people to reinforce each other's ideas and to create a sense of *truth* through social validation. It also allows for the casual peering in and commenting on the perspectives of *others*, enabling reinforcement of the differences between *Us* and *Them*. In this landscape, it takes very little for a comment to be seen as a challenge against a group's beliefs. This, combined with the ease of which anyone can weigh in on a conversation with a written comment, sprinkled with emojis and GIFs, is a recipe for conflict.

People are far more confident that they can accurately interpret someone's intention from the words they have written than they should be. Studies have found that emails from a manager or boss can be interpreted as brief and direct, whereas the same message from a colleague is seen as abrupt and rude. More pointedly for tribal disputes, the mood of the receiver has a massive impact on the interpretation. When we read a comment in anger or with a sense of distrust, we are more likely to interpret it in a negative way. We think we read the intent fairly clearly but in reality, we get it wrong.

As a simple example, consider the following sentence:

'I never said she stole my money.'

Emphasis on the 'I' could imply someone else said it. Emphasis on the 'never' would be a strong denial of the accusation. Emphasis on the 'said' may imply it was thought but never voiced. Emphasis on the 'she' may imply it was someone else. Emphasis on the 'stole' may suggest it was borrowed, whereas a strong 'my' might suggest it was someone else's money that was stolen. Finally, an emphasis on the 'money' might suggest something else was stolen. All this in just seven words. As little as three letters can cause an all-out war on the social media platform formerly known as Twitter. If you don't believe me, try writing 'lol' in the comments section of a serious post of an impassioned group and see what happens.

In the United States, such tribalism led to one of the most extraordinary days in the history of the self-declared greatest country in the world. On 6 January 2021, Congress was set to confirm that Joe Biden had won the election and was to become the next president of the United States of America. However, powered by social media, thousands of supporters of the former president, Donald Trump left their keyboards and rallied in Washington, DC to dispute the decision. Within hours, a mass of furious Trump supporters stormed the Capitol Building, breaching security, destroying property, posing for photographs and clashing with law enforcement. The insurrectionists occupied several parts of the building, some even stalking the corridors looking for lawmakers to do…who knows what. The speed and ferocity of the insurrection was shocking to many. This sort of thing was what happened in countries like Venezuela, Sri Lanka or Libya, but not the United States of America. This powerful movement had been fuelled by the ability for this tribe to share messages and emotions so readily. The whispers of frustration were fostered into sparks of frustration that became a blazing anger within minutes.

Ideological groups have always been a useful haven for humans. Sociologists suggest we have evolved to build and protect these groups as they provide us with important needs: certainty, solidarity and security. In a dangerous world, it is usually safer to be part of a group, even if the beliefs of this group aren't perfectly accurate, than to be correct and alone. Today, we create tribes relentlessly. Be they based on political, religious or moral lies, we are constantly creating noisy groups with the desire and the ability to share and reinforce ideas on a scale never before seen, and this might be just the beginning. That bots and AI might push the influence and drive of tribalism should be of utmost concern to everyone.

Cass Sunstein's brilliant paper, 'The Law of Group Polarization', succinctly collates a range of experiments and analysis to show that not only do group discussions create ideological clusters, but that they also promote a shift to more extreme views by concentrating the type of information, feeding off social proof and labelling the group as an identity. Part of the unwritten obligation of being a member of this group is to defend the group and your fellow group members. If you protect them, they will protect you, further strengthening the group. Trust is fostered, conformity is rewarded and the strength of the group grows.

This group dynamic reinforces further rigidity in our beliefs; strength in numbers leads to hardening of ideas. The more we say it and the more we agree, the harder it is to listen to divergent views. Add to this that the internet is awash with algorithms designed to learn your preferences and steer you towards the information it thinks you will want to see. This personalisation of your social media feed and search results is very useful, but prone to creating filter bubbles that can trap us. If you believe in one conspiracy theory, you will tend to see more and more popping up from your searches. What seemed like a small peripheral issue before can quickly appear to be everywhere and dominating your screens. The more you view feeds, the more you'll be shown in future — it is an ideological prison that can be difficult to escape even if you want to.

To move forward as a species, we must become more skilled at being flexible in our beliefs. I am not saying we need to throw all our beliefs away, nor that we should lack conviction in the beliefs we hold now. Many of the beliefs Sir Isaac Newton held about physics have been proven to be inaccurate. Einstein's theory of relativity and the emergence of quantum mechanics have superseded many of Newton's theories. But this doesn't mean that Newton's work wasn't incredibly useful. For example, classical mechanics — an integral element of Newtonian physics — paved the way for steam engines, aeroplanes and satellites.

Newton's ideas were not dismissed by Einstein. By expanding on the previous ideas and challenging some of the assumptions and conclusions, the theory of relativity enabled yet more innovation into global positioning, satellite communications and nuclear energy. Despite the popularity of Einstein even to this day, he was not completely correct in his theories. While relativity is good at explaining large-scale motion in the universe, it fails at the smallest scales. This led to the development of quantum mechanics by brilliant minds such as Max Planck, Niels Bohr and Werner Heisenberg, among others. Indeed, Einstein himself played a role in developing this new quantum theory.

Quantum mechanics describes the laws that govern the behaviour of particles at the smallest scale where relativity fails. It is based on principles of uncertainty, probability and non-determinism. Quantum theory suggests particles behave in probabilistic ways, and includes phenomena such as entanglement and superposition, which have no counterparts in classical physics. These theories have helped the development of extraordinary technologies such as specific lasers, semiconductors and quantum computers.

To move forward as a species, we must become more skilled at being flexible in our beliefs.

It is also fair to say that these theories don't merge well with each other. Relativity can't explain some of the elements of nuclear fusion, such as quantum tunnelling. Quantum theory, however, can't explain gravity or the observable procession of planetary orbits. Relativity can't explain the Heisenberg uncertainty principle but quantum theory can't explain gravitational time dilation. The list goes on. So, which theory is right?

The beauty of physics, and all good scientific research, is that this question is completely redundant. The objective of scientific research is to use empirical, observable evidence to develop a greater understanding of the workings of the universe. Good science is built in personal objectivity and healthy scepticism. Each year, millions of scientific researchers and professors globally working across an ever-expanding number of fields search deeply for a novel idea they can use to make a name for themselves. If you can prove an existing theory wrong, you are scrutinised carefully for accuracy and, if you are right, lauded for your contributions to the field.

While science is on an insatiable quest for a better understanding, this is not the norm. Most people prefer to feel like they are right and the answer is known rather than being in a state of constant uncertainty and exploration. The normal way people act is to prioritise feeling safe in their beliefs over being curious about possibilities. The problem is, this only ever holds us where we are today. We need more. We must advance forward.

To move us towards better outcomes in the future, we need more people to adopt a scientific mindset. We must be more willing to be wrong. We need to congratulate those who better our understanding in ways we had not seen. We must be willing to let go of what we once thought and embrace with humility the importance of challenging our old beliefs.

Highways and goat tracks

It was late December a few years ago when I found myself staring in horror at the sight in front of me. Soft, flabby and weak were the words that came to mind. I felt sick. The mirror in front of me didn't hold back — there was no distortion or ambiguity. I was out of shape and overweight. After my years of cycling and playing football had been scaled back through running a business, raising a daughter and travelling the world speaking, my body had suffered. Full of embarrassment and frustration, I vowed that the next year would be different. I would start getting up early again and exercising. I'd quit drinking and eat healthy food. No more beers and burgers, which had become almost a staple diet. It was time for change.

Fast forward to March of the following year and I found myself looking up to see my reflection in a window at a local pub. With a burger in one hand and a pint in the other, I remembered the moment from December and realised my best intentions had failed to create any change. Despite how good the burger tasted, I felt a pang of disappointment that I'm sure I'm not alone in experiencing.

Has this happened to you? Research on New Year's resolutions found that while around 40 per cent of people set themselves a promise each cycle of the calendar, only around 8 per cent of people actually achieve their goals. Like me, the vast majority fall back into the same old habits and behaviours that we hoped to change.

The problem is not your personality or willpower, but instead the limitations of the human brain to change through neuroplasticity. Neuroplasticity refers to the brain's ability to reorganise itself by forming and strengthening different neural connections. This adaptive feature of the brain is crucial for learning, developing new skills and storing memories. Everything we think, along with most of the actions we perform, is controlled by the firing of these neural pathways in our brain. Changing our habits, beliefs and mental models depends on this neuroplasticity to help us restructure old pathways while forming and strengthening new ones.

When a certain pathway is fired often, the connections between the neurons, known as synapses, are strengthened. These well-used pathways become akin to four-lane highways in our brains. This reorganisation is useful as it reduces the distance between neurons, meaning less effort is required to fire and making the brain more energy efficient. How amazing is that? Your brain is a self-organising machine focused on using less power. These highways become our defaults and like the social groups reinforcing beliefs, the more we fire a pathway, the stronger and more efficient it becomes.

However, while neuroplasticity enables reorganisation, change and adaptation, it also explains why we humans often find it difficult to change our habits and opinions. Repeated activation is the key to strengthening pathways and creating deeply ingrained neural networks that are optimised for those specific actions or thoughts. This means that breaking a habit requires the slow and often challenging process of weakening old connections and forming new ones. New ideas, actions and habits are also neural pathways within the brain, but due to the lack of firing, these are not like the four-lane highways of our existing pathways. Instead, a new idea is more like a rough little goat track up the side of a hill.

In a moment of stress, pressure or tiredness, the brain is faced with a choice of using the old established mental highway or taking the newer goat track. What we know is that the brain, particularly under strain, tends to prefer the more energy efficient highways. This resistance to the new way is often compounded by cognitive biases such as confirmation bias, where people favour information that confirms their pre-existing beliefs and ignore or rationalise disconfirming evidence.

Imagine this scenario. While eating my breakfast on Sunday morning I feel tired and unhealthy so I make a decision to improve my diet. I pack myself a healthy lunch on Monday, but have back-to-back meetings all day and am feeling run-down. Tuesday morning I forget to pack a healthy lunch and by mid-afternoon am feeling hungry. I need a pick-me-up so I grab a burrito from the takeaway downstairs. In my mind, I justify that it isn't because I don't want to be healthy — I just was busy today. The next day is busy too, and by Friday when someone in my team invites me to join them for dinner after work, I convince myself that I deserve it. By the next Sunday, which pathway has been strengthened: the healthy goat track or the highway to burrito town?

Neuroplasticity provides the brain with remarkable adaptability, but the way it reinforces behaviours contributes to the difficulty of changing established pathways. Overcoming old highways requires considerable effort and persistence. We must persistently take the goat tracks. We need to overcome our instincts and allow the pathway for the new idea, behaviour or habit to be fired over and over again.

Phillippa Lally and her team at University College London found that, on average, it takes about 66 days for a new behaviour to become automatic. While this varies a lot for individuals, the main point is simple: making a change will take persistent effort over an extended period of time. Be persistent in your self-awareness and patient with your regular slips back into old ways. You are only human, after all, like the rest of us.

Trimming the overhanging branches

In our small garden, we have three mature olive trees against the fence with our neighbours. Previously, the neighbour had large palm trees that shadowed these trees from the afternoon sun, but since he removed these palms, the olive trees have gone wild. Their branches now seem to reach over the top of the fence, eager to grab all the afternoon sunshine they can. So, what should be done?

Let's explore three options:

1. Insist the neighbour replant his palms to stop the olive-tree branches from spreading.

2. Pull the olive trees out of the ground.

3. Trim the overhanging branches.

While the choice might seem obvious for the offending olive-tree branches, it's not as clear when it comes to the cognitive branches and beliefs in our minds and in the minds of others. As a gardener, I must tend to my garden. Blaming it on the neighbour or throwing away everything isn't the best answer. If someone's belief doesn't fit with my own, I shouldn't immediately agree with them, nor should I feel the need to impose my view upon them. If I find there is a problem in my beliefs, I can change them. These are my trees; the impetus to change sits with me.

The second option — pulling the olive trees out of the ground — again seems extreme. But this is also how people sometimes see the threat of trimming their ideas. Any challenge to my beliefs could be fatal. People think: if we give an inch here, we might lose the whole thing. This is common in some religious dogma, where desperate attempts are made to explicitly justify every single element as fact for fear that it will reduce the validity of the whole. Did Noah really collect a breeding pair of every animal, put them in a large wooden boat and keep them fed for five months? This story doesn't need to be factually true for the ideas to be valid. 'Noah's Ark' is a story of divine punishment for those with moral decay and how faithful obedience and service can be the path to salvation. Whether you agree or disagree with the underlying moral of the story is a different matter. But trying to convince me that the lions, tigers and hyenas didn't eat all the chickens, cows and sheep for five months doesn't strengthen the moral argument in my eyes.

The answer to my olive-tree problem is obvious. You don't need to pull the whole tree out, just trim the branches. Cut back the offending bits and support the beautiful trees in their ongoing growth. The same should be the case for our ideas, heuristics and beliefs. We should be clear on our moral foundations, our values and the elements we feel are the core of our decision making. But as the world changes around us, don't expect others to change to make our new ideas valid. Don't tell them to change or make them agree. Also, don't think that a challenge to a small part means you have to throw the whole thing out. No, you can and must trim the branches too.

At times, even when we know it deep down, it can be difficult to trim the branches. Admitting we were wrong is hard and is further exacerbated by the social and emotional implications. Being wrong can feel like a personal failure, which can be threatening to our self-esteem and social standing. This is particularly the case in environments and cultures where the pressure is high and certainty and expertise are seen as critical. Frequently, we see case studies from the worlds of healthcare, heavy industry, politics and business that highlight the folly of holding fast onto bad ideas. In these places, admitting wrongness can be seen as a sign of weakness or incompetence.

Take Anatoly Dyatlov. After graduating with honours from the Moscow Engineering and Physics Institute, he worked installing nuclear reactors into submarines. He rose through the ranks of the USSR's nuclear program, fuelled by deep expertise, sharp intellect and a commitment to his work that was noticed by all around him. Dyatlov became the deputy chief engineer of the Chernobyl power plant and oversaw the construction of three reactors that at their peak powered a significant portion of Ukraine. He also played an important role in the development of the safety protocols to protect workers and ensure the safe operation of the facility.

Dyatlov was a demanding manager, intimidating to his subordinates and autocratic in his leadership style. On 26 April 1986, his insistence on proceeding with dangerous testing despite concerns from his team played a significant role in the Chernobyl reactor meltdown. While many factors contributed to this disaster, Dyatlov having more expertise wouldn't have prevented the tragedy. Had he listened to his team or paid more attention to the operational risks, maybe it would have never happened. It is possible that the pressures on Dyatlov from above played a big factor and that the leaders he reported to in his earlier career contributed to the making of the man.

Ultimately, a disaster like this can scarcely be blamed on one man. However, Dyatlov's management style certainly did little to mitigate the impact. His colleague and fellow veteran of the USSR's nuclear program, Vadym Vasylyovych Hryshchenko, summed up that Dyatlov's leadership was based on deep technical knowledge, tireless work ethics and a sullen, dissatisfied nature with other people. He noted that Dyatlov:

> ... *always had his own point of view and never changed it at the request of the boss, he persuaded, did not agree, in the end, obeyed, but remained with his opinion. Similarly, he had little regard for the opinion of his subordinates. Of course, not everyone likes such a person.*

Can you think of someone with these traits? They are not all that uncommon. The ability to admit when we are wrong is crucial for personal growth and learning. It allows us to update our knowledge and adapt to new information, which is essential in an ever-changing world. Acknowledging our mistakes opens us up to new perspectives and deepens our understanding of the world.

It also plays a vital role in maintaining and strengthening relationships. Building trust is a fundamental component of leading with empathy and when individuals can't openly admit their mistakes, trust is eroded. We must be humble and admit that some of our ideas are wrong without fear of judgement or reprisal. This will encourage more open communication and foster a culture of updating ideas around us.

Building a culture of branch trimming is beneficial to ourselves and the relationships we hold, allowing for more open and collaborative environments to flourish. Fostering an environment that encourages admitting wrongness can lead to more robust decision-making processes and innovation. In our modern, complex and volatile world, we need groups of people who embrace this principle fully. You and your team will be constantly bombarded with new information and changing circumstances. Trimming the ideological branches will be vital for sustainability and growth.

Ultimately, becoming better at admitting we are wrong is not just about correcting individual mistakes; it's about cultivating a culture of curiosity, openness and resilience. Embracing our fallibility with humility can reduce conflicts, enhance decision making, and promote a more compassionate and understanding society. It encourages us all to remain learners, humble and wise in the recognition that knowledge is vast, and our grasp of it is always incomplete.

CHAPTER 5
Leading with empathy

Decision making is hard, but as a leader it is not an option; it is an essential duty. In the words of Theodore Roosevelt, 'In any moment of decision, the best thing you can do is the right thing, the next best thing is the wrong thing, and the worst thing you can do is nothing'.

Leaders must navigate through the complex landscape of challenges, opportunities and responsibilities, making choices that often have far-reaching implications for many people. Avoiding decisions, or delaying them, can lead to stagnation, missed opportunities and even catastrophe. It is vital to understand that the role of a leader inherently involves making tough decisions, sometimes under pressure and with incomplete information. This is where empathy can help. By gathering more information, we can make better decisions.

There are countless examples of situations where indecisive leadership caused significant harm. In 2014, the Australian Department of Human Services had been exploring ways to better identify people who had underreported their incomes and claimed more welfare support than they should have. A concept was developed called the Online Compliance Intervention. The idea was to use annual data from the Australian Tax Office to automatically calculate potential overpayments and issue debt notices. This avoided the slow, staff intensive process previously in place.

In initial meetings, Department of Social Services personnel flagged that this system seemed flawed. Questions were raised as the system would even begin debt recovery procedures and reduce future payments before the person could appeal the decision. Internal advice documented the validity of these concerns: the proposal didn't align with policy and was unlawful.

However, a few weeks later, the system was presented to the Minister for Social Services boasting an estimated $1.2 billion in savings. The then Minister, Scott Morrison signed off on the initiative. The desire to crack down on people rorting the system and the juicy financial savings seemed to have been strong enough to quiet all the concerns.

What a Royal Commission later found was a long list of individuals who while being concerned about the initiative, succumbed to incessant pressure to implement quickly and realise the savings. Many people knew it was wrong. Not enough were willing to push back against the Ministers' excitement.

The system was implemented mid-2016 followed almost instantly by complaints from both welfare recipients and frontline public sector staff. There were reports of confusion, psychological distress and a lack of support from those being notified of often incorrect debts. By early 2017, media outlets were reporting flaws in the system, sharing the stories of vulnerable people being harassed and even links between debt notices and suicides. However, the new Minister for Human Services defended the scheme, and it continued.

During the next two years concerns about the system only grew. Senior officials were informed that the scheme's methods were likely unlawful, and the Ombudsman even issued a report highlighting flaws. Still, it took until November 2019 before the Government conceded in the Federal Court that their scheme, now known as Robodebt, was legally and ethically wrong. The scheme was then terminated and the processes for compensation and a Royal Commission begun.

This wasn't a failure of process, data or policy, this was a failure of leadership. As Commissioner Catherine Holmes shared in the final report:

> There was clear awareness among senior public servants and ministers of the distress and harm caused by the scheme well before any action was taken. Some acted with dishonesty, others with wilful blindness.

As a leader, if you are not taking action when issues emerge or are identified, you are effectively incentivising people to continue doing the wrong thing. Ignorance in leadership is unacceptable. While people will likely point the finger of blame at the most senior person they don't like, the failure of leadership came from far below the Ministers. As unpopular as it might have been to challenge the desires of a man who would later become the Prime Minister of Australia, everyone needed to do so much earlier.

In early 2017, Rhys Cauzzo, a young florist from Melbourne, received a notice through the scheme stating he owed more than $28 000. The notice was later found to be incorrect, but that was all far too late. Internal systems had flagged Rhys as a vulnerable person, but the scheme seemingly ignored this. He was contacted more than two dozen times by officials and debt collectors. In testimony to the Royal Commission, his mother, Jennifer Miller described how the relentless harassment and aggressive tactics put huge pressure on Rhys, leading to a deterioration of his mental health. Rhys took his own life, yet Robodebt continued for almost two more years.

Were the leaders just ignoring the concerns raised? Did leaders know and not care? Did they fail to ask the questions as to the human impacts of the scheme? Were they simply too focused on the big numbers to see the individual stories? I don't really know. But what is certain is that the government failed Rhys.

Decisions create ripples, but silence and indecision often create the deepest wounds. Ignoring the human elements while maintaining a focus on dollars had clearly blinded many within the departments and hundreds of thousands of Australians felt the stress, pain and anxiety as a consequence. You will need to make decisions at times that some people don't like. You might have to call things out and take an unpopular stand. Sometimes this will frustrate the people closest to you.

This is why effective decision making requires gathering not only factual and quantitative data but also emotional and intangible insights. Empathy plays a crucial role in this process. Understanding the emotions, motivations and concerns of all people involved and impacted can provide a fuller picture of the situation, leading to more informed and balanced decisions.

Consider a leader deciding on a restructuring plan. Beyond analysing financial reports and performance metrics, they would be wise to engage with employees to understand their fears, hopes and suggestions. They explore the impacts on customers, other partners and stakeholders. They should consider the impact the change will have on the culture, and the benefits and risks should be mapped thoroughly to support the success of the change. This approach may uncover hidden issues and opportunities, allowing them to craft a plan that is not only effective but also considerate of the organisational culture.

You might have to call things out and take an unpopular stand. Sometimes this will frustrate the people closest to you.

What if they don't like me?

Early in my consulting career, I had the chance to work with someone who was simply a brilliant leader. At the time, he didn't actually have the title of leader. We were peers in a team, but he was certainly wiser and more experienced than me and most of the other people in the team. Steve was a talented consultant but an even better people leader. I learned so much during those early years on managing stakeholders, handling conflict and finding solutions when everyone else was ready to give up. Steve and I formed a friendship on top of work, regularly grabbing a beer after work or cycling around Sydney on the weekends.

It was more than 10 years later that I would reunite with Steve. He was working to build a new team and needed some good consultants to help deliver the work. I jumped at the chance! However, after just a few months, I knew this wasn't the right role for me. This put me in an awkward position. I really liked Steve and knew he needed people to grow his team, but I also knew that my staying there was the wrong move for everyone involved. I just didn't know how to tell him.

I asked Steve for a meeting and he agreed. He suggested we go to a café rather than a boring meeting room. After sitting down, I was immediately feeling nervous about how to say something that I knew Steve didn't want to hear. The waiter came over to take our orders and bought me a few seconds. Once the waiter left, Steve turned to me and said, 'Just so you know, our friendship is far more important to me than any job'.

It was like a line out of a movie, perfectly timed and worded. Steve had obviously known that I wasn't happy and that while my decision to leave would be a challenge for him, it was the right thing to do. He also likely observed that I was feeling nervous and a little guilty about having to leave, and he made sure this wasn't the focus of the conversation. This was a masterstroke in empathic leadership.

As Steve highlighted to me so brilliantly, our friendships and personal relationships should exist outside the decisions we make on specific issues and topics. Making a decision that my friend doesn't agree with doesn't mean I like my friend any less than before. Moreover, your decisions as a leader should be based on your best judgement using the data and information you have at your disposal. They shouldn't be swayed by the opinions of friends who don't have the same level of information or responsibility for decision making. If they have valuable information, yes you should listen and incorporate that into your decisions. Just don't let their opinions overwhelm the decision-making process based on your relationship alone.

One of the most challenging aspects of leadership is accepting that no decision will satisfy everyone, especially those closest to you. In the case above with Steve, my decision was not ideal for him, but he accepted it and used the opportunity to reiterate how much he valued our relationship, which lives on strong to this day. Leaders must develop resilience around decision making. A strong sense of self-assurance is required to navigate the inevitable dissent and dissatisfaction that will be felt, and often voiced, by some people when a decision is made. Role modelling this level of acceptance and resilience is a critical element of a leader.

It is essential to communicate openly and honestly, explaining the rationale behind decisions and acknowledging the concerns of those who disagree. Empathy helps deliver these challenging decisions more gracefully and with greater clarity as it supports the alignment of the decision drivers with the uncovered needs, desires and beliefs of the people we are communicating with. By genuinely understanding the various stakeholders involved, leaders can explain decisions in a way that mitigates feelings of resentment and fosters a culture of respect. This does not mean everyone will be delighted. It will also not eliminate conflict. It can, however, transform what can be hidden resentment or underground politics into more constructive dialogue, where differing viewpoints are acknowledged, explored and valued.

In this way, empathy is a powerful tool for fostering trust and understanding, both before and after decisions are made. When leaders take the time to connect with their team members, understand their perspectives and engage their views in the decision-making process, it fosters greater acknowledgement and respect.

Leading with empathy transforms not only the way leaders make specific decisions but also the way they see the world. Empathetic leaders are more aware of the impacts of their decisions on various stakeholder groups as they have invested the time to better understand them, sometimes on numerous occasions or for significant amounts of time. They become more skilled at understanding others and more attuned to different stakeholder perspectives. Empathy allows us to build relationships beyond rapport. It allows us to build deep, trusting relationships that can be the catalysts for transformational change.

One powerful example of leading with empathy is Daryl Davis. As an African-American blues musician who travelled and played in bars throughout the Deep South of the United States, Daryl had every reason to fear, avoid and despise anyone associated with the Ku Klux Klan (KKK). However, instead of letting hate be the fuel of ongoing fires, Daryl led with empathy and embarked on a remarkable journey of reconciliation and understanding.

Instead of avoiding KKK members, Daryl engaged with members of the white supremacist group to start conversations and even friendships. His approach was unconventional yet profoundly effective. Rooted in conscious curiosity, open exploration and a commitment to challenging entrenched thought models, Davis was able to look beyond the white hooded veils of hatred and prejudice to connect with the individual people and their own stories, fears and vulnerabilities.

Many of his encounters would begin in unexpected ways. A chance conversation after one of his performances or a casual conversation at a bar. When many of the KKK members disclosed their affiliations and beliefs, Davis resisted the urge to respond in anger. He instead chose to listen to these individuals with curiosity and kindness, seeking to explore the deep roots of their racist beliefs. Listening attentively to their concerns and patiently building trust over time, Davis was able to establish a genuine human connection with people who initially saw him only as the colour of his skin.

One of the most notable examples of his impact was his friendship with Roger Kelly, a former Imperial Wizard of the KKK. Davis had to overcome Kelly's initial suspicions around Davis' intentions but over time came to respect and admire him. Their friendship so deeply challenged Kelly's long-held and ingrained racist beliefs, he was forced to make a change internally.

Roger Kelly renounced his ties to the Klan and publicly apologised for his past actions and hateful impact. This transformation underscored the power of an empathic approach. It is conversations, connection and understanding that help us break down the barriers of prejudice and foster reconciliation in a fractured world. As Daryl says himself, 'When we choose to listen instead of judge, we create space for empathy and understanding'.

Through his work, Daryl Davis demonstrates that we can't just fight fire with fire. Confronting others with condemnation or confrontation does little other than to cement the battle lines for further conflict. Empathy, patience and a willingness to engage with those who hold different, even prejudiced and hateful, views provides greater opportunity for everyone to walk away in a better state than before. By humanising the 'other' and challenging stereotypes through empathic exposure, Davis showed that meaningful change is possible, but it sometimes happens just one conversation at a time.

Do good people just do good things?

In 2008, I was working for the Commonwealth Bank of Australia and had been invited to a dinner for leaders within the finance division. At the dinner, a gentleman named Peter Baines got up to speak to us after our main meal. This moment changed the direction of my life. Peter told of the tragic circumstances of so many young children following the 2004 Boxing Day tsunami. He talked about the charity he had created to raise money and build homes for the children who had lost their families during the catastrophe. Given I had had an experience I will share later in this book, I committed instantly to support Pete. In the following 16 years, I journeyed to Thailand more than 30 times. Sometimes we were cycling hundreds of kilometres in a charity ride. Other times I journeyed there to spend time with the kids in the homes, teach English and organise the scope of works for repairs on the homes.

One thing that certainly changed in my many times to the land of smiles was the way I saw the world. Time after time, I saw situations where I had clear, Western expectations of what would happen next only to see them completely shattered. One particular moment stands out. It was on a 1600-kilometre bike ride that started in the north east of Thailand. One day on this ride, I stopped at an intersection of two dirt roads in the middle of nowhere. Across the road, I saw a family of four sitting under a small bamboo hut eating their breakfast on woven mats. Their tiny home was a makeshift collection of wood and iron, and the rusty motorbike in the yard seemed their only mode of transportation. It must have been quite a strange sight for this family. Western tourists were rare in this part of the world, let alone ones clad in Lycra on a bicycle. I had probably spent more on my helmet and sunglasses than they made in a year and here I was stopped in front of their home like an alien had just beamed me down from space.

The father of the family stared for a few seconds before waving his hand and yelling 'kin khao'. Kin khao translates literally to 'eat rice'. He was inviting me to come and join his family for breakfast. I was stunned. Imagine the reaction I might receive if I was to pull up on a bicycle in front of a home in Sydney or Melbourne where a family was sharing breakfast. I suspect the reaction would range from suspicion to ignorance. I certainly doubt they would invite me in for bacon and eggs. This family with almost nothing was willing to share what little they had with a complete stranger.

It would be easy to suggest that he was a kinder, more trusting and generous person than me. I am sure that I wouldn't have greeted a weirdly dressed stranger at my door with the same offer. Maybe it is more accurate, though, to say his mental models for this situation were possibly kinder, and more trusting and generous than mine. I can't speculate too much on how this man would have treated other people in my position. Maybe if I was an ordinary Thai person on a motorbike, he may have acted differently. If I was dressed in different clothes, if I was a different ethnicity or gender, he may have not made the same offer. I can't say for sure. He may have had a particularly good morning for some reason and his good mood shaped his response. Maybe he treats all people in the same way. I'll never know.

The question of whether his response was good or not almost misses the main point. The better question would be whether his response was useful or not. From an early age, we are taught to look for the right answers to questions. We experience this in examinations in school and universities. We are posed with questions and are told to find the right answer. However, in the real world, there is rarely an objectively correct response. More often we are given limited amounts of information and asked to make a time-sensitive decision from an almost endless number of different alternatives. While many people will insist we chose the wrong answer with the wisdom of hindsight, the reality is, our decisions are often an attempt to navigate the ambiguity of the world with our best judgement. And at times we get it wrong.

Instead of judging the goodness or badness of a decision or action, let's instead focus on how we make these decisions and what control we have over the reaction or response process.

Do you react or respond?

Imagine you have been struck down by an acute pain in your stomach. You find yourself doubled over, slumped in a doorway. Unable to move, you would be waiting desperately for someone to walk by and assist you. You might imagine it would be lucky for you if this not only occurred on a visit to Princeton Theological Seminary where students were walking past, but that many of these students had just been studying the text of the Good Samaritan.

The Good Samaritan is a biblical story of a man who is attacked by robbers and left injured on the side of the road. A priest and a Levite both pass by without helping, but a Samaritan, considered an outsider, stops to assist him. The Samaritan tends to the man's wounds and takes him to an inn, paying for his care. This parable teaches the importance of compassion and helping others, regardless of their background or social status.

Of the large number of students that were going to be walking past you, half of them had actually been studying this story to deliver it in a lecture that very day. You'd probably think there would be a pretty high chance that someone who was walking to a class to give a lecture on the Good Samaritan would stop and help, right? This was what researchers John Darley and Daniel Batson were looking to test in their famous 1973 study.

They brought together a group of students who had either been preparing a presentation on the text of the Good Samaritan or a talk on the career of a minister. They instructed the participants to walk to a lecture hall across the campus to give their presentations. To get to the lecture hall, they would walk straight past a person slumped in a doorway in pain. Darley and Batson wanted to find out if the students would stop to help based on the type of presentation they would be giving. Surely someone who was focused on the story would be more likely to stop than someone who was thinking about the general life as a minister?

Somewhat surprisingly, they found no difference in the likelihood of stopping based on the type of talk they were prepared to give. Instead, something else caused a dramatic change in the likelihood of them stopping. The best predictor was whether they were in a hurry. Of those who were told to head to the lecture hall without any time pressure, 63 per cent stopped to help the person in distress. However, when they were told they needed to hurry across campus to deliver their talk, the percentage of people who stopped plummeted to just 10 per cent. Despite having studied a text specifically about helping someone in this exact type of situation, 90 per cent of them hurried straight past without stopping.

When we consider how we make decisions, it's easy to think of our interactions with the world as a simple combination of action and reaction. Someone does something and we react. We face a situation and we react accordingly. However, this ignores the important step in between the stimulus and our response: we must interpret the situation. We take in information and data about the specifics and use this to understand what is going on before we choose our response.

While interpretation is a complex system of neural networks, a simple way to consider our interpretation is through two lenses: our mental models and our mood. While walking past the injured person, two-thirds of the participants in Darley and Batson's experiment interpreted the situation they faced as one where they should take action to help. We could assume their mental models for offering help were triggered and they acted. However, when they felt rushed, their mood overwhelmed their attention and they interpreted the situation differently.

Maybe they didn't see the injured person at all. When our emotions take hold, our focus of attention shrinks and it is easy to miss things we would have otherwise been influenced by. We become more unconsciously reactive and seemingly less in control of our actions. While we might have mental models that would interpret the situation in a kind or generous way, that doesn't mean we will always access them. Our mood will shape where we place our attention and potentially which models will be used.

This is why it is so important for leaders to be conscious of their emotions, particularly when the environment is stressful.

The natural biological reaction to stressful situations is an anxiety response. This typically includes increased heart rate, suppression of the digestive and immune systems, and rapid breathing, all of which occur to prepare us to fight or flee danger. However, along with these physical responses, the brain also increases levels of cortisol, which impairs the function of the hippocampus, impacting memory and learning. This in turn reduces concentration, impacts decision making and increases levels of pessimism.

Research has established a strong link between anxiety and pessimism, indicating that these two psychological states often reinforce each other. Anxiety, characterised by excessive worry and fear, can lead to a negative bias in thinking. This negativity can foster a pessimistic outlook, where individuals consistently anticipate the worst outcomes. Studies have shown that anxious individuals are more likely to focus on potential threats and negative possibilities, which perpetuates a cycle of worry and pessimism. When you are in a funk, clouds seem to lose their silver linings.

While self-awareness and personal stress management can be effective, research has also shown that interventions targeting anxiety can also reduce pessimism. Those struggling should look to support in the form of cognitive behavioural therapy (CBT), which addresses cognitive distortions and promotes healthier thinking patterns. By learning to challenge and reframe negative thoughts, we can reduce anxiety levels and adopt a more balanced, optimistic perspective. This therapeutic focuses on the intertwined nature of anxiety and pessimism and highlights the potential for positive change through targeted psychological interventions.

One of the most critical actions we need to take when we feel our elephants start to get agitated and emotions are building is to look to engage the rider. Bring conscious awareness to your emotions, become curious as to why you are reacting the way you are and ask yourself a question: Will this emotion be useful for me in this situation?

Sometimes emotions like anger and frustration can be useful—that's part of the reason they exist. However, too often we let the elephant lead the dance with its emotional reaction rather than consciously considering all the information and choosing to respond. There is a big difference between reacting and responding.

In his masterpiece *Man's Search for Meaning*, Austrian neurologist, psychiatrist and Holocaust survivor Viktor Frankl describes the difference perfectly. While observing fellow inmates in the Nazi concentration camps, Frankl noticed that it wasn't just the horrific conditions that predicted their survival. Despite the disgusting and dehumanising conditions, those who found purpose and meaning maintained greater mental and physical health.

As Frankl writes in *Man's Search for Meaning*, 'Between stimulus and response there is a space. In that space is our power to choose our response. In our response lies our growth and our freedom'. It is unlikely you will have to face the horrors that Frankl and his inmates met—hopefully no-one will ever again. However, you will face challenges. There will be tough times and you will be tested. Stress will rise around you and even inside you. The question is not whether you can avoid it, but how you choose to respond. This is your freedom.

CHAPTER 6

Influencing and inspiring through empathy

It was lunchtime at school and I was super excited. I was about 14 years old at the time and I had just picked up from the tuckshop a parcel of culinary beauty. It was a white bread roll stuffed with roast chicken, hot chips and gravy. It was a delicacy that they rarely made at the tuckshop and coming from a poor family, I could rarely afford it. But on this day, the stars had aligned and I found myself sitting with my group of friends, a massive smile across my face and about to shove the roll into my salivating mouth.

Just as I was about to take the first bite, a friend of mine touched me on the shoulder. I turned to see her staring at me with a disappointed look on her face. She began to berate me for eating the roll, going into detail describing the number of chickens that die each year, the horrible conditions of the farms and the suffering that millions of farm animals endure just so cruel people like me can eat things like the roll I was holding in my hands.

I was immediately annoyed by her finger wagging and chastising over my lunch for three reasons. First, I was 14 and it was lunchtime so I wasn't really interested in thinking about anything. Second, I was deeply in love with this bread-encased goodness and she was trying to come between us, and finally, I was pretty sure I'd seen her eating a hot dog the week before! Notwithstanding it could be argued that there are pretty limited amounts of meat in a hot dog, they are still made of some animal parts, aren't they?

Thinking through the Empathy Process can illuminate the trap that my friend, and many of us, regularly fall into. Clearly, my friend had become consciously curious about animal rights. She had then openly explored, reading books, articles and gathering other information about certain farming practices. She had then challenged and changed her mental model. Her old mental model saw eating meat as normal and now this had shifted to seeing eating meat as horrible and cruel. She was then in the space of leading with empathy, making decisions about what she would and would not eat based on this new interpretation of the world. All of this makes perfect sense.

The trap she fell into is that she now thought the best action would be to directly challenge my mental model. I can assure you that in this example, it was completely ineffective. I ate the chicken roll. The only thing that changed was my relationship with my friend. This approach of telling people they are wrong and trying to change their minds by overwhelming them with information is too often completely ineffective. Think of a time when you were told, out of the blue, that you were wrong about something. How did your elephant react? If you are like most people, an aggressive rebuttal of something you believe will be treated as a threat.

When our ideas are challenged, particularly when we see these as important to our social standing, it can trigger an activation in regions of the brain associated with rejection. I'm sure you have had the experience before of challenging someone's idea or opinion and then seeing a noticeable defensive reaction follow.

When our ideas are challenged, particularly when we see these as important to our social standing, it can trigger an activation in regions of the brain associated with rejection.

At that time, their brain will react with an anxiety response akin to the one I had. This will reduce cognitive function, debilitate memorability and restrict their ability to learn. By telling someone they are wrong, we are effectively making it much harder for them to listen and change their mind.

What I'd type but never say

Despite the ineffective nature of this approach, it is incredibly common. Everyday, thousands of posts on social media are showered with comments by people spouting their opinions as correct and dismissively claiming any other view as incorrect. Online, people write to each other through social media and chat boards in ways that you would never dream of doing in person.

Analyses of social media conversations have shown what I'm sure most people will have witnessed themselves and need no empirical studies to show: people on social media are much more hostile, aggressive and certain of their opinions than they generally are in public. Social media removes one of the most important and immediate sources of feedback in communication: the other person's face. Without being able to see the other person, we can more easily demonise, dehumanise and attack anyone online within the relative safety of our internet anonymity.

Look at these 'conversations' from a popular social media site:

User A: We need to stop letting these criminals into our country. They're taking our jobs and ruining everything!

User B: You're an ignorant bigot! Immigrants contribute more to this country than you ever will. Educate yourself!

User C: Both of you are idiots. The real issue is corrupt politicians using immigration to distract us from their failures.

User A made a statement that was clearly disagreed with by User B. Rather than seek to understand User A's position, User B immediately attacked both User A's idea and their personal character. What would you say is the probability that after this comment from User B, User A became more curious about the point they were making and openly explored the internet and other sources for additional information on the topic? Pretty close to zero, I suspect. Maybe their point on the social benefits of immigration is perfectly valid and one that User A had not yet considered or researched in detail. However, after being paired with personal attacks, its influence has been watered down if not tainted by the toxicity of their approach.

When User C entered the comments, I had some hope for a mediation of sorts. Alas, this was not to be. Instead, User C simply added new information and insult into the discussion. By immediately attacking both Users A and B, there would be little chance of a useful and curious exploration of their points either. The most common path for a triad such as this will be a constant barrage of personal attacks, often sprinkled with a set of facts, beliefs and assumptions from each that purely back their own point of view and fail to acknowledge or rebuke any of the views of the other two. A descent into chaos is the likely outcome.

Here is another exchange from a social media thread discussing the famous photograph 'Earthrise'. In this classic image taken by astronaut Will Anders during the *Apollo 8* mission in 1968, the reflective planet Earth is seen rising above the horizon of the moon in its spectacular vibrant colour. While many have said this is one of the most inspiring and influential images ever taken, highlighting the beauty and fragility of our planet, in recent years it has become a symbol of furious debate. Here is one exchange. Although the names have been altered or removed to protect contributors' identities, it highlights how quick people are to jump in and fight for their ideas.

John Jones: Check out this article that proves the Earth is flat: Flat Earth Proof. Don't let NASA fool you!

Jane Swan: John, are you serious? This 'proof' is just a bunch of pseudoscience. The Earth is round, and there's plenty of real evidence to support it.

Mark Peters: Jane, have you even looked at the article? It has some valid points. Why do you blindly trust everything NASA says?

Emily Davies: Mark, it's not about blindly trusting NASA. It's about trusting centuries of scientific research and evidence. The curvature of the Earth has been proven in countless ways.

Tom Wills: Emily, have you ever been to space? No, right? So how can you be so sure? All we have are images and data provided by agencies that have a vested interest in keeping the truth hidden.

Laura Whiting: Tom, that's ridiculous. We've had independent verifications from various sources, including private space companies. The evidence is overwhelming.

Peter Browning: Laura, you're missing the point. Why is it so hard to believe that there could be a massive cover-up? Governments lie all the time.

Alice Green: Peter, the sheer scale of such a cover-up would be impossible to maintain. Thousands of scientists and experts from all over the world would have to be in on it. It's just not plausible.

Sam Allen: All of you are idiots. How can you be so blind to the truth? The Earth is flat, end of story. Wake up, sheeple!

Tom Larrimer: Flat Earthers are just too stupid to understand basic science. Go back to school and learn something, morons.

Alex Chen: Why are we even wasting time on these brain-dead conspiracy theorists? They should be banned from the internet for spreading lies.

The only thing sadder than the inevitability of the outcome is the frequency of it occurring. While social media might show us many obvious examples of this toxic discourse, it is not a new phenomenon. There are also famous examples in the past of poor communication and confrontational approaches having poor results with sometimes fatal consequences.

Wash your hands, you grub

My daughter Zoe loves *Bluey*. If you haven't seen it, *Bluey* is a brilliant little cartoon show about a family of Australian dogs called the Heelers. It is a short yet beautifully written series of cartoons that wrestle with many of the more common challenges parents and kids face growing up, with a classically iconic Australian spin. The influence of *Bluey* has extended far beyond the boundaries of the land down under. There have been reports of children in the United States using the terms 'brekky' and 'dunny'—Australian colloquialisms for breakfast and toilet—due to watching the show.

In one episode, Bluey says to her dad, Bandit: 'Ya big grub'. It's a term I use towards my daughter regularly, especially when I want her to wash her hands. One day as she was applying the soap and running the water, she asked, 'Dad, why do we need to wash our hands?'

I replied it was to wash off the germs so we don't get sick.

'Why don't dogs need to wash their paws?' she responded, pointing to our groodle who was studiously watching guard.

I said that dogs were different from people and they don't get sick from the same germs as we do.

'Can germs make us dead?' Zoe asked.

'Some germs can make you very sick and maybe you can die, so we wash our hands just to be safe,' I replied, hoping that would appease her. I was wrong.

'What sort of germs are the bad ones?' she continued to dig.

'Well, there are some very dangerous germs. They are especially around things like dead animals. Remember I told you not to touch the dead bird we saw in the park? They have really bad germs. But it is best to wash your hands anyway, to keep them clean'. She wasn't satisfied.

'Really? I don't think germs are that bad,' Zoe retorted.

'Did you know that, a long time ago, people didn't know about germs at all? There were some doctors who would work with different types of sick people and because they didn't wash their hands, people got very sick and even died in hospitals,' I told her gently. 'Washing your hands is very important, honey; it is to keep you safe.'

'Okay Dad, I'll wash my hands.' She scrubbed the soap between her fingers before rinsing her hands with the water.

What I find interesting about this exchange is that not only is it true that people die in hospital, but also people who should know better are even less receptive to the idea than Zoe. In 1847, Ignaz Semmelweis was working as an obstetrics assistant at the Vienna General Hospital. He observed that the rate of death following childbirth was significantly higher in the hospital than expected. At the time, almost one in five women who gave birth in the clinic would develop puerperal sepsis, or childbed fever. The condition was almost always fatal.

This was not a new condition. Lady Jane Seymour, King Henry VIII's third wife, had died of the condition some 300 years earlier. However, Semmelweis observed that the mortality rate was vastly different between two of the wards. While the ward attended by medical students recorded high rates of up to 20 per cent of women developing childbed fever, another ward only staffed by midwives had a rate closer to 2 per cent. Semmelweis became curious as to the difference — then one incident sparked his great hypothesis.

During an autopsy, a colleague, Jakob Kalletschka, accidentally cut himself. He quickly developed symptoms consistent with childbed fever and died. Semmelweis hypothesised that because the medical students were performing autopsies on bodies, they might be carrying 'cadaverous particles' from these autopsies into the delivery rooms, causing the infections. He instituted a policy of handwashing in the hospital using a chlorinated lime solution, which reduced the rates of childbed fever from almost 20 per cent of all births to less than 2 per cent.

At this point, the trajectory of the story looks straightforward. Semmelweis should publish his findings, be lauded throughout the world as a medical pioneer, offered prestigious roles at hospitals across Europe and see his handwashing protocols reduce childbed fever across the globe. Sadly, this is not how this story goes. Despite the clear success, Semmelweis' ideas were met with strong resistance. Many colleagues and superiors were sceptical or outright hostile towards his suggestions that the deaths were being caused by medical students and professionals.

Two years later, he was let go by the Vienna General Hospital. He took a role as head physician of the obstetrics ward at St Rochus Hospital in Hungary, where he implemented his handwashing practices with similar success. In 1861 — a full 14 years after his initial findings — he published his work in a book titled

The Etiology, Concept, and Prophylaxis of Childbed Fever, but it was not well received by the medical community. Four years later, Semmelweis was committed to a mental asylum. His health deteriorated rapidly and he died soon after, largely dismissed and maligned by his peers.

It wasn't until almost 30 years later that — based on the work of Louis Pasteur, Robert Koch and in particular the influence of Joseph Lister — germ theory and the practice of hand washing was widely accepted. So why did Lister succeed where Semmelweis failed? The answer is not whether one was more correct. They both had sound concepts regarding the role of tiny particles in causing childbed fever. Both thought the washing and disinfecting of hands was crucial and both had tested their ideas with success. So, why was Semmelweis shunned but Lister accepted?

The answer has a bit to do with the empathy gap: Semmelweis was an abrasive and confrontational character. Deep passion for his work often translated to disdain for those who didn't agree. He was erratic, harshly criticising colleagues and even superiors who were naturally sceptical of his new, revolutionary idea. Rather than gather support for his theory, Semmelweis accused senior physicians and professors at the hospital of negligence. His arguments often veered from the professional into personal attacks of character. Semmelweis held senior physicians directly responsible for the high mortality rates, an accusation many clearly denied. This combative style and an inability to work with peers directly led to his dismissal from the Vienna General Hospital.

In contrast, Joseph Lister had much greater success for a number of reasons. First, his work built on the previously accepted findings of Louis Pasteur on germ theory and disease. He also demonstrated more scientific rigour in his testing and analysis. But one of the critical differences in Lister's approach was likely the most impactful. Rather than being focused on his own conviction and desire to be right, Lister focused on methods to ensure he and his colleagues got the right outcome. Lister did not blame the physicians directly, but focused on the bacteria he was looking to stop. By initially sanitising equipment and patient wounds, he took the focus off the dirty hands of those he looked to influence and into a space everyone could look to with curiosity.

As discussed, when looking to influence others, we need to be incredibly sensitive to triggering their elephant. It's hard to change another person's mind, especially when they see themselves as experts. Ego and expertise are powerful forces to be challenged directly. As Upton Sinclair famously said: 'It is difficult to get a man to understand something, when his salary depends on his not understanding it'. By pointing fingers at the equipment and not the physicians, Lister created opportunities for even sceptical colleagues to curiously explore the data and implications. It may well have been the case that the mental illness that saw Semmelweis committed was also responsible for his irritable demeanour. However, it is hard to imagine just how many women perished needlessly during childbirth between his findings and the eventual acceptance of the importance of hand washing.

Care more about them than about being right

Unlike Semmelweis, we may not have to try and influence stubborn physicians of their culpability in the deaths of thousands of women, but we are always influencing. As the speed of change in the environment continues to accelerate, so grows the need for us to be able to influence people around us into different ways of seeing, thinking and acting in the world. As a leader, you will almost certainly have new ideas to seed, new perspectives to explore and new strategies to rally people around. Some will be welcomed and almost insignificant; others will feel like a sudden U-turn for very heavy and otherwise happy elephants.

In order to not fall into the trap that Semmelweis did, we need to reframe what is truly important. Too often, people experience a deep sense of significance in their own beliefs, especially when they have a passion fuelled by a recent journey of discovery and transformation. You can only imagine the passion Semmelweis had when he saw the rate of mortality drop and mothers walking out of hospital with their babies rather than being wheeled out in a casket. When we have wrestled and battled the old ideas in our mind, it is easy for the passion to build. We have overcome an old version of ourselves and birthed something new, powerful and magnificent. It is like a baby we want to protect and let flourish across the world. Any rejection is an attack we must defend.

This is not to say we shouldn't challenge the beliefs of others — indeed this is a critical act of leaders. We will regularly be required to question the current ideas in order to shape a better future. Much of leadership is the act of rallying and coordinating people to move in a new direction, one that may require them to change their existing ideas and take on new ones. How do we solve this paradox? People don't like to have their ideas challenged but we must do so in order to lead them. We know that the common approach of factual overwhelm doesn't work, but what does? Sir David Attenborough may have discovered one answer to this question.

Next to Morgan Freeman, Sir David Attenborough might have one of the most recognisable voices in the world. During a career spanning 70 years, he has made more than 100 documentaries that blend spectacular cinematography, accessible scientific information, and an engaging and emotive narration that turns the natural world into a gripping story the whole family can explore with wonder and awe.

In his documentary *Planet Earth II*, we see the drama of nature in all its grandeur. In one of the most incredible scenes, a baby iguana hatches on the Galápagos Islands to be confronted with the need to race over rocky terrain, avoiding a horde of hungry racer snakes desperate to feast on the newborn reptile. As the skilled camera operator follows the tiny iguana, snakes chasing and striking at it, your heart races with hope for the tiny lizard, with Attenborough guiding us through every exciting leap from rock to rock.

It's hard to imagine too many people giving a thought for baby iguanas in the Galápagos Islands before this episode. Maybe, few even gave it too many thoughts after. But in this moment, we are captivated by the scene in front of us. We watch with wonder, fully engaged and emotionally invested. We are filled with curiosity and explore the perspectives and ideas shared with an openness that wishes only to know more. Sir David Attenborough deeply believes that everyone should care about the environment. But the approach he uses to influence people is not to simply tell them. It is not to berate, belittle or accuse them of not caring enough. He doesn't want to force us to care, he wants us to truly care.

This is the true path to influencing others without telling them what to think. We must inspire curiosity so the people we want to care actually care. If you tell a child to like another because you say they should, how do you expect they might act towards that child? My suspicion would be somewhere between begrudgingly complying or surreptitiously despising them. We can't force people to care. They have to want to care. They must be interested to care. The path Attenborough uses, and the one that the Process for Empathy recommends, is to inspire curiosity in others.

Much like the first step in the process, we want those we are looking to influence to be consciously curious. While it is challenging to do, inspiring curiosity provides us with an opportunity to create a willingness for people to park their existing beliefs and spend time in deliberate and open exploration. While we might not have the cinematic masterpieces at Attenborough's disposal, the aim should be to use the elements at our disposal to inspire thoughtful curiosity before all else.

While travelling through Argentina in 2006, Blake Mycoskie became concerned with the struggles of children walking to school with no shoes. He wasn't the first to see the children with cuts, scrapes and scars on their feet. He wasn't the first to learn of the soil-transmitted infections that regularly impacted the kids. He wasn't the first to learn of the social stigma and indignity these children faced in their communities when others wore shoes. He wasn't even the first to want to do something about it.

While many people would buy shoes for a few children, this was neither a sustainable nor scalable solution. There were millions of children around the world who would need new shoes as their feet grew and shoes wore out. The question Mycoskie asked was one that could inspire curiosity in others: 'What if every time you bought a pair of shoes, a child in need received a pair too?' This simple question sparked curiosity in the minds of others. Why wouldn't they do this? It seemed so simple.

Out of this simple idea, TOMS Shoes was born. Its buy-one-give-one model was simple, but this simple and inspiring question created clarity for consumers and investors alike. The initial instinctive designs meant others asked questions of people wearing the shoes and the simple mission allowed conversations to flow. Since bootstrapping TOMS in 2006, Mycoskie has taken this simple question from a spark of inspiration to generating hundreds of millions in annual revenue. More importantly, TOMS has provided more than 100 million pairs of shoes, restored the sight of nearly 800 000 people and provided clean water for hundreds of thousands of communities across the globe.

While a good orator can captivate an audience with eloquence and charm, it is the person who inspires curiosity who creates a spark within the listener. This is the magic that can lead others to become consciously curious, to question deeply, explore openly and ultimately discover new ways to see the world. Don't tell — instead, evoke the wonder within.

CHAPTER 7

Building an empathic organisational culture

Have you ever been in a meeting with your boss and they didn't quite perform as you'd have hoped? Maybe they were disorganised, unprepared or didn't meet your expectations in their input. What would you do? I've asked this question of hundreds of people and the most common responses I receive range from saying nothing to complaining to other staff about their performance, but almost no-one says they would actually tell their boss directly. Many would call this too dangerous: a career-limiting move that would only end badly for them.

What about not only telling the boss, but telling them very bluntly in an email? This is exactly what Senior Portfolio Strategist Jim Haskel did. In 2013, after a research meeting that included the boss, Jim sent a scathing email directly to him. This wasn't just Jim's line manager in a large hierarchy. Jim's boss was the founder, chairman and chief investment officer of the largest hedge fund in the world: Ray Dalio.

The email read:

Ray—You deserve a 'D–' for your performance today in the meeting. You did not prepare at all, because there is no way you could have been that disorganised. In the future, I/we would ask you to take some time and prepare ... but we can't let this happen again.

How do you think an email like this would be received by some of the managers you've had in the past? How would you respond if it was sent to you?

In response, Ray Dalio did something out of the ordinary. He read the email, then typed an apology reply that acknowledged the feedback and requested that the management committee investigate the incident to ascertain if it was part of a pattern of behaviour requiring additional action. But his reply didn't just go to Haskel — Dalio forwarded the original email and his reply to the entire company.

Ray Dalio believes in radical transparency, a management philosophy that advocates for complete openness and honesty within an organisation. It implores people to embrace critical feedback and openly challenge the ideas and behaviours of others. At Bridgewater, no-one is immune to criticism. Dalio's response was role-modelling this philosophy with pure humility and he wanted everyone to see. Radical transparency can foster a strong sense of trust, accountability and continuous improvement within a group, but it is not for everyone. Most people are not used to this level of candour and tend to allow issues to dwell in the dark corners, sometimes fading without consequence and other times festering into bigger challenges.

I would love to recommend you implement this philosophy of radical transparency in your team immediately — but maybe a word of caution. Opening the floodgates of feedback can overwhelm people not accustomed to this environment. It can also allow for some to use this as an excuse to bully and belittle others, which, while it is not within the philosophy's principles, happens all too often. Some teams will have massive issues with fostering a sense of confidentiality and even suffer emotional stress.

It is also not this radical transparency alone that drives Bridgewater's success. Dalio has instituted an idea meritocracy, meaning the best ideas always win, no matter where they originate from. Everyone is obligated to provide ideas, speak up and challenge ideas that have been raised by anyone. Thoughtful disagreement is not avoided, it is demanded.

Bridgewater also spends significant energy on clarifying goals and measuring progress. Everyone is clear on the direction they are driving in and when the data suggests they are off track, they adjust. It isn't enough to simply know which way they are heading. They are also all committed to pushing each other to get the best results.

Before we make a leap, it is worth considering what foundations exist within our team and how we can strengthen them first to grow a culture of empathy, transparency and excellence.

From a team of rivals to an unrivalled team

Building a high-performing team is a challenge and maintaining it is even harder. When you bring a group of humans together with all their complexities and nuances, they form a unique way of doing things and a feeling about the group. This is their culture and it never remains static. The Greek philosopher Heraclitus said, 'No man ever steps in the same river twice. For it's not the same river and he's not the same man'. The water is constantly flowing, changing and shifting the sand, pebbles and sticks. Many days may be calm with little change; other days heavy rain or other events will transform the river rapidly. The same is true

When you bring a group of humans together with all their complexities and nuances, they form a unique way of doing things and a feeling about the group.

of each of us as people. We can have many consecutive days with only small changes, then the next day it can all fall apart. The culture within a team, group or organisation changes constantly and often in very asymmetrical ways.

That is why when we look at group culture, like that illustrated in figure 7.1 (overleaf), it is much more common to see cultures form that sit towards the bottom half of the chart. It's not that people set out to intentionally develop internal rivalries and self-destruction; it's just the law of entropy. Things tend towards disorder. It's difficult to develop the behaviours and commitments needed to become an unrivalled team and even harder to maintain these high and demanding expectations. When something starts to slip, the downward spiral can be swift and hard to stop.

The lowest rung on our ladder is the team of competitive rivals. There are many reasons a group can develop into this destructive state. Often, misaligned goals and objectives can push people to create competing priorities. Inconsistent leadership and poor feedback can also play a role, as can a lack of purpose and clarity on responsibilities. The common feature of this level is that people are generally focused on personal survival.

You will hear such teams say 'keep your heads down' or 'don't rock the boat'. Terms like these speak to a dangerous environment where people are concerned with safety rather than achieving outcomes. Without psychological safety, aggressive behaviours — particularly in management — such as bullying, undermining and pressuring colleagues can flourish. These will often be accompanied by their more passive counterparts of avoidance, ignorance and defensiveness. Bureaucratic organisations will begin to fill with formal processes of communication that rely on rules over trust. Self-destruction becomes almost inevitable as activity slows, productivity fades and pressure for results intensifies.

CULTURE	FOCUS	PERSONA	OUTCOME
Constructive challengers	Deep trust and accountability	Committed leader	Adaptive high performance
Cooperative collaborators	Group cohesion	Supportive squad	Consistent execution
Comfortable compliance	Completing tasks	Valley of apathy	Mediocre results
Solo mavericks	Individual results	Ego-driven pirates	Disconnected chaos
Competitive rivals	Personal survival	Avoidant passengers	Self destruction

UNRIVALLED TEAM ←⟶ TEAM OF RIVALS

Figure 7.1: group culture

The level above this, where I experience the cultures of many groups of salespeople and highly technical folk form, is one of solo mavericks. Here, people focus a lot on getting the work done, but are really only interested in their own work. Results are a badge of honour to be shown off and the goal is to be the best. Whether it is to make the biggest numbers, design the best solution or complete more than anyone else, the focus is on individual excellence — sometimes at the expense of the group.

This creates a platform for internal competition, often fuelled by leaderboards, bonuses and accolades for individuals rather than group results. In this environment, pride can overcome purpose and negative behaviours can become the norm to 'win at all costs'. At best, these highly competitive environments create a relentless pressure for results that will have short-term benefits but in the long term lead to a chaotic mess. At its most dangerous, a solo maverick culture can become a breeding ground for unethical behaviour. This culture drove Enron to great heights before a disastrous collapse. It led Wells-Fargo employees to open fake accounts to meet targets, despite harming customers. It drove Volkswagen engineers to install software to falsify emissions testing results.

Many groups are happy to reach the safe haven of comfortable compliance. Here people are content to complete the tasks required of them and call it a day. The environment is typically nice enough and people tend to avoid confrontation more out of apathy than fear. Apathy can become a dominant feature of such workplaces, with terms such as 'ride it out' and 'it's just a job' becoming strong signs that people see the bare minimum as the standard to strive for.

The challenge for a group stuck in comfortable compliance is that the world around them is more ambitious. Quickly, the old ways of doing things become uncompetitive. 'Just good enough' products or services are superseded by competitors and preferred by customers. Mediocre results are not acceptable in the eyes of markets or shareholders. Demands are increased on the workforce, sometimes with a sweeping change of upper management and performance target ultimatums. Under this pressure, many comfortably compliant workplaces struggle to adapt and can descend into competitive rivals focused again on survival alone.

The exception too often is within government and not-for-profit organisations where the demands of shareholders don't impose the same dynamic forces. Bureaucracy thrives in comfortable compliance with people actively developing policies, rules and processes to slow down the flow of change and maintain the status quo. Rather than embracing the challenges of the world around, the comfortably compliant seek to ignore it, often dragging down any newcomer with fresh ideas. There is a laundry list of promising political figures and successful corporate leaders who have tried to reform bureaucratic groups only to have their efforts drowned in an apathetic quagmire.

To move beyond the comfort of compliance — which they must do to sustain performance and thrive in our modern, complex world — they must become more cooperative, collaborative and cohesive as a group. This requires members of the group to develop greater trust and understanding for each other and the work they do. It is not enough to complete your tasks and hope that some master plan will mean it will all work out. The volatility in the external environment will produce problems full of uncertainty and ambiguity that require people to work together to solve.

This is where the Empathy Process becomes the linchpin for truly high-performing teams. A prerequisite of true collaboration is that each person understands what they are trying to accomplish, what the other person might also be looking to accomplish and how our ideas together can support a positive outcome. This understanding is challenging when people are so busy and focused on their own complex area and is best established through conscious and deliberate curiosity for other people: supportive and open exploration of perspective, ideas and desires that might be similar to or completely different from our own. Through exploration we create shared understanding and mental models that are more effective in the decision-making process. It is leading with empathy as a team sport.

If that sounds a little too easy, you might be wondering why it isn't the norm in organisations. Why do so many struggle to rise above and create a culture of collaboration? The answer is simple. If people don't care, they won't bother asking. The valley of apathy we create in teams has a powerful effect on our behaviour. The comfort of safe silence must be overcome by active curiosity. People must reach out, be proactive in their approach and seek information from others. They have to care enough about the outcome they are striving for to do the extra work. They have to fight against the inertia of apathy — and this takes something vital. They must have trust.

When nothing is wrong, maybe everything is wrong

Harvard Professor Amy Edmondson was conducting a field study at eight hospital units to determine the impact of psychological safety on the frequency of errors reported. First, she asked team members a series of questions to identify their levels of comfort in speaking up, interpersonal trust and mutual respect. This provided a data point as to the level of psychological safety in each team. She then interviewed staff members and formed a hypothesis that higher levels of psychological safety would lead to fewer errors and better patient outcomes.

When she uploaded the data on the errors reported in each team, she thought it must be wrong. Not only did the level of psychological safety not reduce the number of errors, but it seemed to drive them up. The greater the level of trust and understanding, the more errors. While this might seem counterintuitive, it is actually exactly what you would want from a medical team.

Imagine you are going to hospital for an operation. While fairly routine, there are always risks involved with surgery and so you do a little research on the number of incidents the hospitals have reported in the past year. Hospital A has had three risk incidents, hospital B has had 47 and hospital C has had zero. Which would you choose?

A natural response might be the one with zero incidents. Why would you choose a hospital that had 47 incidents when the others are lower? In reality, people may be unlikely to choose the hospital with 47 incidents because they feel it must have serious issues in the way it operates. But this is entirely misleading. When working in complex environments, incidents can and do happen regularly. This is just a fact. How many they report is not as much an indication of the risks in the environment as much as the culture of the team who are working in it.

Take the case of Deepwater Horizon. This vessel, slightly bigger than a football field, operated with 126 people aboard. It was capable of floating more than two kilometres above the ocean floor and drilling wells deeper below the surface than Mount Everest is high to extract oil. The Deepwater Horizon crew worked in incredibly hazardous and volatile conditions. However, they had reported zero lost-time incidents for the seven years leading up to the catastrophic events of April 2010. Managers from BP and Transocean were aboard the vessel at the time of the disaster celebrating their stellar record. No lost-time incidents is a good thing, right? Wrong.

Despite the crew not reporting any lost time, the US Coast Guard had investigated 16 fires and other incidents, issuing 18 citations to the vessel between 2000 and 2010. In 2008, 77 people were evacuated when a section of pipe was removed incorrectly, causing the platform to partially sink. Internal BP documents showed concerns around the equipment used on the platform and that pressure from management wanting them to meet targets contributed to the explosion. Despite this, the lost-time reporting submitted to the regulator by the operators was spotless.

The real problem with the Deepwater Horizon was the culture that had been formed. It was highly competitive and people were not willing to speak up for fear of retribution. Crew members reported viewing safety tests as box-ticking exercises. They looked for ways to do the task and move on. Data was siloed and poorly communicated, if communicated at all. When people don't have the trust and psychological safety to speak out, they will happily slide into the comfort of the valley of apathy. Sadly for them, their errors led to one of the greatest man-made ecological disasters in history.

Amy Edmondson's research found when psychological safety is high, teams are more focused on the outcomes than their egos. They are open to discussion, collaboration and challenging each other to find better solutions. Particularly when trust is built between members of a team, they become more committed to shared success than personal glory.

Herding elephants into trust

Thinking back to our model of the rider and the elephant, trust is not built through a formula by the rider; it is felt by elephants. It is a question of whether the elephant feels safe. This is why empathy plays such a critical role in both the development and maintenance of trusted relationships. Building deep, trusted relationships within a team is one of the most vital aspects of effective leadership. While your level of trust might be most important in times of errors and crises, the value and importance of building trust must be viewed as a constant practice for and between all team members. Trust expert Rachel Botsman emphasises that to build deep trust, we must create a sense of closeness and understanding among individuals. We need to display curiosity, authenticity and vulnerability in our interactions.

Ascending from cooperative collaborators to constructive challengers is a dangerous step unless elephants feel safe. Empathy fosters deeper relationships, as it involves understanding and appreciating other perspectives — and appreciating them regardless of your own views. When individuals empathise, they are more likely to consider other members of the team before taking action and considering others' needs in the process. Understanding the nuances of your team members' behaviour, their mental models and underlying motivations helps maintain more accurate sets of expectations, increasing a sense of certainty and better predicting their actions, which in turn fosters greater trust.

CHAPTER 8

When the robots start to cry

Over my decade-long exploration, I always worked on the assumption that computers could never match humans in the field of empathy. I looked at characters such as Sheldon Cooper from the series, *The Big Bang Theory*. This robotic personality seemed unable to understand the nuances of human emotion in the people around him. It wasn't that he was an evil character; this lack of understanding seemed to be inherent in his DNA. He just was born without empathy.

I came to suspect that there are many people like this, myself included. We can imagine a sliding scale of empathy in each person and indeed many tools — such as the Hogan Empathy Scale, Perth Empathy Scale and Toronto Empathy Questionnaire — provide users with a score of their empathic capabilities. In my mind, one end was home to the incredibly intuitive, natural empaths. People like my late Nana, who seemed to know what you were feeling before you and were so in tune with what others were experiencing. At the other end of the scale was me, Sheldon and many people I have encountered who feel they just weren't born with it. But as part of this spectrum, I had assumed that even those down my end would always be superior at empathising compared with the cold, hard motherboards of a computer. Right?

In 2023, a group of researchers decided to put this idea to the test. Using a now seemingly ancient version of OpenAI's ChatGPT released in November 2022, they wanted to know how a large language model would compare against humans in providing both accurate and empathic answers to medical questions. The data they used was from Reddit's AskDocs forum, a place where people can post medical questions that are then answered by verified healthcare professionals.

Almost 200 original questions from the site were fed into ChatGPT and its responses were reviewed along with the original human responses by a panel of licensed healthcare professionals. However, the panel wasn't told which of the responses were from a person and which were from the AI. Their task was to rate each answer on the basis of quality of response and the empathic nature of the response. Turns out, ChatGPT's responses were rated as not only more accurate but also far more empathic!

Another study assessed ChatGPT on the Levels of Emotional Awareness Scale, a test of the ability to recognise and describe emotions. Again, the AI significantly outperformed human baselines in both emotional awareness and in its accuracy at identifying emotions. It appears that AI will not only make its way onto the empathy spectrum, but it is also a far superior tool for understanding and empathising with people.

The applications of this technology are incredible. A few years ago, I had an issue with my internet provider. I contacted their call centre to ask for support and waited on hold for more than 30 minutes before a human answered. Already frustrated, I tried to explain the problem I was having but before I could finish my first sentence they cut me off.

'Let me stop you. I need your name and account number first,' they said with clear frustration in their own voice. I responded with the details and started to continue with my explanation of the problem before they again said with a raised voice, 'Stop, stop, stop. This is a business account. You've come through to the wrong area. I'll transfer you. Just stay on the line'.

There was a click, followed by the annoying hold music once again. I was now angry. I waited for another 15 minutes, all the while stewing about the rude treatment I had been given. Adding to the frustration was the automated messages suggesting I can go online to self-service my problems. Hardly a useful message when you are calling due to your internet connection not working!

Eventually, the music stopped and a new voice introduced themselves with the following:

'Hello, this is Alex. Can you please start with your full name and account number?'

By this point my frustration was palpable. I read out my account number, followed by my name, as I had already done before.

'Great. Can I also get your four-digit business PIN?' Alex said in a now annoyingly chirpy voice.

'I don't have a business PIN. Well I'm pretty sure I don't. I've never set one up. I just need my internet fixed,' I said, trying my best not to explode in fury.

'I see. Can you tell me your postal address and the mobile number attached to the account?' Alex asked. I shared the information requested through clenched teeth.

'It looks like you have one of our older modems,' Alex continued. 'Can you tell me the serial number on the bottom?'

'What? Why? It's the device you sent me. It's not working and I need it fixed.' My emotions were now getting the best of me. Alex didn't appreciate it.

'I'm sorry, sir. If I don't have the number I can't look up the codes. If you don't have the number you might need to find it and call back. Have a good day.'

The line went dead. Alex had hung up the phone. My blood boiled.

Many of Australia's largest companies claim customer service as part of their vision and values. Medical equipment giant ResMed says they are 'customer obsessed'. National Australia Bank has an ambition to be Australia's and New Zealand's most customer-centric company. Optus says that customer focus is a major priority. Even major gambling company Sportsbet says it puts 'customers first and last'. I won't challenge the degree of conviction the senior leaders held when signing off on these statements. However, even assuming they are deeply genuine in their desires, realising these ambitions is impossible without thousands, if not millions, of consistent actions by every member of their large workforces supported by systems and processes to execute.

It's hard to imagine the future of customer service not being driven by AI. Not only will it be used to ensure customer interactions are more consistent through complex customer journeys and more personalised utilising existing customer data, but also by creating AI agents that are potentially superior at both empathising with customers and not being negatively influenced by the reactions and emotions of the customer. In my scenario above, our hypothetical AI agent wouldn't have needed to forward me on, ask for any details or become frustrated with my responses.

It's likely that my contact centre interaction will become extinct within the coming years and if that is the case, bring on the robots. The improvement we will be able to achieve in so many aspects of life with AI is set to revolutionise the globe. Dario Amodei, CEO of Anthropic, the makers of ClaudeAI, has speculated that it will be akin to the next industrial revolution for humanity. There will be so much opportunity to take frustrating, repetitive and even dangerous work off the plates of people to be handled by robots that are efficient, effective, self-improving and even empathic. This sounds like utopia in the making. What could possibly go wrong?

Are we building monsters?

Wisdom is a gift so often delivered in strange wrapping. While exploring the potential impacts of AI, I've been amazed, but not surprised, at the acceleration in people using tools such as ChatGPT and Copilot to rapidly automate tasks and speed up our everyday work. While browsing through Disney+ with my daughter a while ago in the never-ending search for what she 'really wants to watch', we stumbled across *Fantasia*, which was released in 1940. I was keen to see if Zoe would appreciate the old-school cartoons backed by classical music.

Needless to say, her review of the first few minutes was pretty clear: 'This is boring!' However, we persisted... well, *I* persisted. After winning her back with the lure of dancing fairies, we settled in to watch probably the most memorable of all the scenes of the film. Enter Mickey Mouse as the sorcerer's apprentice. Mickey, tired of carrying buckets of water for his sorcerer master, decides to don his sleeping master's hat and use magic to bring a broomstick to life to carry the water for him. Initially, the plan seems to be a stroke of genius. The broomstick diligently carries the buckets, following Mickey to the well and back, delivering the water in time with the rhythmical score. Mickey now rests in a chair, enjoying his time to relax, while the broom completes his loathsome chore, and slowly drifts into a peaceful sleep.

Mickey begins to dream of the wonderful things he could do when he becomes a sorcerer: making the stars shoot across the sky and burst into a shower of fireworks; controlling the waves, the clouds, the thunder and the heavens. However, his dream is rudely interrupted as he wakes to find himself floating in waist-deep water. During his slumber, the diligent little broomstick had continued to carry buckets of water, filling the cauldron until it had overflowed. Even then it continued as the water ran down the stairs and lapped against Mickey's chair. It worked so hard that now the room was flooded — and it showed no sign of stopping.

I wondered, is this us in modern times? Are we so quick to outsource our tasks to AI tools and busy ourselves with other tasks that we fail to keep track of what is happening? In 2017, Facebook researchers developed AI chatbots designed to handle negotiations. In testing them against each other, the researchers found the chatbots stopped using grammatical or recognisable English, instead creating shorthand language only the bots could understand. This increased the efficiency of the chatbot negotiation, but also left the researchers with no ability to understand what was going on.

On 1 August 2017, the BBC reported one of the exchanges between the bots, named Bob and Alice, as follows:

Bob: i can i i everything else.............

Alice: balls have zero to me to me to me to me to me to me to me to me to

Bob: you i everything else..............

Alice: balls have a ball to me to me to me to me to me to me to me

The researchers shut the bots down. Fortunately, this has caused no harm to Facebook or its billions of users... well, not yet anyway.

When YouTube's algorithm was maximised for user engagement in 2018, it didn't create a new language, but it did change the behaviour of people and the shape of society more broadly.

In an effort to increase the value of YouTube, the AI was programmed to find ways to increase users' watch time. The more people watched, the more ads they would see. More ad views is more ad revenue, so it made perfect sense for the AI to search for ways to keep people engaged. Maybe a little unsurprisingly, it found that content that was sensational, controversial and emotive was the best to keep people watching. As the AI ramped up the extreme dial, people became more fixated.

Quickly, people who were looking for cat videos would receive suggestions to watch more violent or politically charged clips. In Brazil, the algorithm found that extreme nationalist content was keeping people watching and so served it up on autoplay to millions. A 2019 *New York Times* investigation found that YouTube's autoplay recommendations heavily promoted far-right and conspiratorial content. A wave of far-right influencers were transformed from just a small voice to the dominant face of users hooked on their sensationalist videos. This not only boosted YouTube's ad revenue, but also played a large role in the rise of Jair Bolsonaro from a marginal figure in Brazilian politics to becoming the president. His polarising presidency was marked by weakened environmental protections, strong nationalist rhetoric and deep political divisions.

Like Mickey, the team at YouTube had asked the servant to complete a simple job, and it completed it diligently. The number of monthly active users on YouTube grew from 1.5 billion in 2016 to 2.5 billion in 2021 while advertising revenue jumped from $6.7 billion to over $28 billion in the same period. The mop filled the buckets, but sadly the unintended consequences were much worse than a mild flood in the sorcerer's castle. The 2021 Mozilla Foundation report titled

'YouTube Regrets' compiled the data of more than 37 000 users from 91 countries who shared their regrettable experiences on the world's largest video platform. The three major findings of this research were that:

1. while the content concerns reported were varied, they were consistently disturbing. From political misinformation to sexualised remakes of children's cartoons, the regrettable moments were often a mix of violence, graphic content, hate speech, scams and other inappropriate content being auto played for users who never searched for it

2. the algorithm was pushing the regrettable content. More than 70 per cent of all the reports were about content recommended by YouTube, much of which was unrelated to the users' previously watched videos. This included several instances where the recommended videos actually breached YouTube's own community guidelines

3. it was worse for people in non–English speaking countries. While YouTube had a group of people reviewing videos — and even looked to hire an additional 10 000 human moderators after this information surfaced — the vast majority were from English-speaking countries. The Mozilla Foundation report found the regrettable results were 60 per cent higher in countries that don't use English as a primary language. Brazil, Germany and France reported particularly high numbers and pandemic-related misinformation was especially prevalent in non-English languages. When it comes to the subjective world of interpretation, localised context can be very important. An impassioned political speech might seem harmless if you don't speak Portuguese and disturbing if you do.

There is no way to know the precise global impact of the algorithm. This was a unique time in our history with a global pandemic pushing many viewers indoors and onto their screens searching for answers. I can't imagine it was challenging for the algorithm to find controversial content to share, but how much was its creation and dissemination accelerated by the hunger for advertising dollars? How many people were radicalised by content they didn't search for? How responsible is the algorithm for the Christchurch mosque attack in 2019 where a gunman killed 51 people and claimed that far-right content on YouTube influenced his actions?

I wonder, if we thought of this YouTube algorithm as a god instead of a computer, would we view it as evil? If the algorithm were instead a team of people sitting in a room and actively recommending the same videos for users, would we not be outraged at these people and their actions? Wouldn't we be demanding some repercussions and responsibility? What if it were a single person plotting, scheming and calculating that it's worth a little collateral damage to the world if they can make billions of dollars more — wouldn't we imagine them as a Bond villain living in a mountain on an island shaped like a skull?

This is where the AI threat becomes challenging. While it can deal with many of the tasks we don't like to do with more efficiency and effectiveness than any human, what are the risks? I don't see the risks being the jobs it will displace, but in the unintended consequences created by poor instructions, unclear goals and our failure to foresee the chaotic outcomes inherent in the large and complex systems. While YouTube claims to have changed elements of its algorithm, there is still criticism and debate regarding the impact these large platforms have on our behaviour. YouTube might clean up its act under governmental and regulatory pressure, but what about iQIYI, Youku, Kuaishou,

Dailymotion, MX Player and Vimeo, who, combined, have more than two billion monthly active users? These other platforms are each small today compared to YouTube, but if implementing a similar algorithm might dramatically increase their active users, is there not a massive temptation to try something similar to grow the share of such a lucrative market?

In *Fantasia*, Mickey finds himself unable to stop the water-carrying broomstick, eventually taking an axe to the magical broom. To his horror, each of the splintered pieces comes alive, sprouting arms and carrying more buckets of water, relentlessly continuing their task until our apprentice wizard is drowning in a spinning whirlpool of water flooding the castle. It isn't until the sorcerer himself returns that the spell is broken, the water cleared and Mickey returns to his manual labour of fetching water himself.

This wise tale provides us with ample caution. When we deploy AI to support our efforts, we must not fall asleep assuming that it will do tasks the way we expect. Sometimes AI will be a perfect fit and work brilliantly to deliver the outcomes expected. Other times it will achieve the intended goal but the collateral damage in doing so may be unexpected and unacceptable. There will also be times where the actions, computations and decisions AI is making will be outside of our ability to understand. We have already seen examples of AI making decisions that seem incomprehensible. In 2016, Google's AlphaGo was playing the ancient game Go against the grandmaster Lee Se-Dol. At one point, AlphaGo made a move so unexpected and surprising that Lee Se-Dol had to leave the room to regain his composure. The AI went on to win the tournament 4–1, dispelling the long-held assumption that unlike chess, a computer couldn't master the complex tactics of Go.

The big question for us as humans in the world of AI will not be what it can solve, nor even how. It will be who is accountable for the outcomes.

The big question for us as humans in the world of AI will not be what it can solve, nor even how. It will be who is accountable for the outcomes.

Those dogs were going to hurt somebody one day

In 2001, Dianne Whipple had just picked up some groceries and was heading home to her apartment in Pacific Heights, San Francisco. At the same time, her neighbour, Marjorie Knoller, was leaving her apartment to take her dog, Bane, for a walk. Bane was an imposing animal. He was a 60-kilogram Presa Canario, a breed known for its large build, confident temperament and protective nature.

As Whipple approached her door, Bane lunged at her, knocking her to the ground. Knoller, unable to control the hulking animal, watched in horror as Bane mauled the defenceless Whipple. Her desperate screams caught the attention of Knoller's other dog, Hera. Also a large Presa Canario, she pushed her way out through Knoller's apartment door and joined Bane in the attack.

Whipple was rushed to hospital but the blood loss and trauma were too great. An autopsy found the dogs inflicted 77 bite wounds on Whipple and severed her jugular. Knoller was charged with second-degree murder, involuntary manslaughter and owning a mischievous animal that caused death.

Majorie Knoller's husband, Robert Noel, was also charged with involuntary manslaughter and owning a mischievous animal that caused death. Knoller and Noel, who were both lawyers, insisted in their defence that the attack was unexpected and accidental, and that Whipple may have even provoked Bane in some way. Knoller also insisted that she was simply unable to stop Bane and Hera in the moment of the attack.

This was a tragic, complex and controversial incident. A first trial found Knoller guilty of all charges and sentenced her to 15 years in prison and her husband Noel to four years. Two years later, an appeal successfully reasoned that while Knoller had acted recklessly, there was no proof she intended to cause Whipple's death or knew the attack would be fatal, seeing her sentence reduced to just four years. However, the California Supreme Court reviewed the case and found this second judgement to be incorrect.

The Supreme Court found Knoller had been warned of the danger her dogs posed to others, knew they had attacked people before and subsequently failed to take basic precautions to mitigate the risks her dogs posed. Moreover, her lack of remorse for the victim and her claims that it was Whipple who was partially responsible for not closing her door was taken into account when reinstating her 15-year prison sentence.

In the future of AI, this incident might be an incredibly important case. While it might be more challenging, could you argue that YouTube's algorithm was partially responsible for some of the terrible human behaviour that was attributed to it by the perpetrators? What about when the actions of the algorithm are much more direct?

Just because we don't know why an algorithm took a certain action, does that mean no human is responsible for the damage it causes? It has echoes of the US National Rifle Association slogan: 'Guns don't kill people, people kill people'. Will this be the same when it is AI doing the killing? While there are increasing calls for regulation and control of AI, its proliferation into every area of our lives is unlikely to slow down. The genie is out of the bottle and it's unlikely anyone can put it back in. We can't stop the AI, but we must better understand ourselves first.

This is why we so desperately need more empathy right now. Having a greater understanding of the people around us, the impacts our actions could have on others and whether these impacts are ethical are all still human accountabilities. We must carefully think about the systems and scenarios we deploy AI within. We need to understand more, and not just the technical aspects, but also the ethical impacts. Unlike our friend Mickey, there might not be a sorcerer coming down to save the day. I suspect we will have to live with the outcomes that our AI tools deliver and hope that, unlike the broomstick, we will be able to switch them off when it goes awry.

It is my hope that empathy will provide us with some buffer to this potential danger. While we are typically good at anticipating the positive impacts that our efforts might have on people like us, the better we can get at anticipating the impacts these actions might have on people very different from ourselves will determine the damage we cause.

At subsequent parole hearings, Knoller has expressed regret and remorse for her failure to prevent Whipple's death. However, this is little comfort for Whipple's family and friends. The world of AI will not only present new dangers, but will accelerate their impact in ways we've never seen before. Today is the day we all need to be more human. Today is the day we need to commit to having more empathy, not just for those on our side, but for all people. While we invest heavily in developing artificial intelligence, we need to also invest in being empathically human.

CONCLUSION
The hardest skill we learn

As we've seen, it requires a lot of effort to put aside our own concerns, park our assumptions and beliefs, halt the pursuit of our own goals and simply focus on someone else. It takes considerable time to have meaningful conversations, to openly explore and to reflect conscientiously on our own mental models. In a world where everyone is busy all the time and calendars are packed with back-to-back meetings, it can be easy to see empathy as a soft skill that is a luxury for people with time on their hands.

I believe the effort is worthwhile and will create lasting impact, but don't just take my word for it. CEO of Microsoft, Satya Nadella has spoken extensively on the importance of empathy in both leadership and innovation. In an interview, Nadella asserts that 'empathy is not a soft skill. In fact, it's the hardest skill we learn — to relate to the world, to relate to people that matter the most to us'. He sees empathy as a 'necessary condition to create great solutions that are profitable and competitive'. Nadella sees effective collaboration as the key to modern work and empathy as the skill we need to foster in order to supercharge this collaboration.

We must have empathy for those we serve to better understand their needs. Empathy for our peers, our partners and our pains in the butt. It does take a lot of individual effort. Empathy and understanding is not something easily outsourced. Moreover, even if you could get a perfect report of all the nuances of another person, it isn't the same as being empathic ourselves. Imagine someone you have never spoken to before, someone you don't know who seems to 'know you'. While they might be very accurate, how would you feel about them?

The byproduct of leading with empathy is that we build trust with people. This trust is one of the magic ingredients that fuels team culture and performance. It is the time we invest in understanding people that builds the trust we need to succeed. Many leaders want their teams to be passionate about their work. To really care.

Why should they care about their work if you don't care about them?

In a world of automation, artificial intelligence and big data, humans will need empathy more than ever to build trusted bonds. Former president of the United States, Barack Obama once said: 'Empathy is a quality of character that can change the world'. Now is the time we need you to lead with empathy and ensure that change is meaningful and positive for your team.

Printed and bound by CPI Group (UK) Ltd, Croydon, CR0 4YY

14/07/2025

14702804-0001